SHREVEPORT MARTYR
FATHER JEAN PIERRE

T0356450

SHREVEPORT MARTYR
FATHER JEAN PIERRE

FEARFUL STEPS STRENGTHENED BY HOPE

Very Reverend Peter B. Mangum, JCL
William Ryan Smith, MA; Cheryl H. White, PhD
Foreword by Christophe Cardinal Pierre, Apostolic Nuncio to the United States
Translations by Audrey Garrett

THE
History
PRESS

Published by The History Press
An imprint of Arcadia Publishing
Charleston, SC
www.historypress.com

First published 2025

Manufactured in the United States

ISBN 9781467155441

Library of Congress Control Number: 2023946791

Notice: The information in this book is true and complete to the best of our knowledge. It is offered without guarantee on the part of the author or The History Press. The author and The History Press disclaim all liability in connection with the use of this book.

This work is dedicated to the memory of Father Jean Pierre,
Servant of God and Martyr to his Charity (1831–1873).
Father Pierre accurately foreshadowed his own self-sacrificial death in an 1858
letter to Bishop Auguste Martin by refusing a respite from his priestly duties
during an outbreak of yellow fever in Shreveport. He offered to his bishop the
explanation that he could not abandon his people.
"I would fear that by my leaving, Catholics would die without the
sacraments.…I would rather die twenty deaths on the battlefield."

CONTENTS

FOREWORD

The history of my homeland of Brittany, France, bears out the historical reality that the Catholic faith has been its greatest export. Countless numbers of zealous missionary priests have embarked on spiritual and geographical journeys that traversed oceans and continents to answer the profound and selfless call to serve God's people in distant foreign lands.

Such is the poignant pilgrimage related in the following narrative that recounts the life of a heroic priest and distinguished scholar, destined to die a martyr to charity in a remote frontier town of Louisiana. Here we encounter but one of the heroic priests who gave their lives in the service of charity in Shreveport, Louisiana, in 1873. The five Shreveport Martyrs—Father Isidore Quémerais, Father Jean Pierre, Father Jean Marie Biler, Father Louis Gergaud and Father François Le Vézouët—answered the summons of Bishop Auguste Marie Martin, a native of Saint-Malo. It was an answer that led to their free and willing offering of their own lives to live out the Gospel for the many they encountered in hours of greatest need.

Shreveport Martyrs of 1873: The Surest Path to Heaven, published in 2021, relates in full the story of all five of these virtuous priests. This volume, however, focuses on the life of just one: Father Jean Pierre, from the small Breton village of Lanloup, who came to the new mission field of the Diocese of Natchitoches in 1854. Through his own letters, the reader confronts the often harsh realities of nineteenth-century life in rural Louisiana for one so determined to minister as a priest in a largely Protestant population. Father Pierre worked among the people of God without regard to their religious identity or social standing, relating to all of us a model of simply being present to serve those around us. He was a beloved community leader, teacher, scholar and generous benefactor of Holy Mother Church, but ultimately, it is his steadfast decision to lay down his own life in a time of great human crisis that is at the core of this remarkable story.

Father Jean Pierre, founding pastor of Holy Trinity Church in Shreveport, is the heartbeat of a story that has endured for over 150 years. His memory lives in the annals of history, in community memory, in beautiful stained glass and in the prayers of the faithful to this day. Because of meticulous research into his life for a Cause for Beatification and Canonization, the pages that follow breathe ever-new life into an already honorable legacy. From the rugged landscape of Brittany to the frontier woodlands of northern Louisiana, Father Pierre's journey resounds with eternal triumph. His journey, like those of so many of missionary zeal, is a testament to the enduring power of faith in the face of mortal danger. When confronting the end of his physical life, Father Pierre saw it as his ultimate offering to God, as an act of perfect love.

May Father Jean Pierre and the other Shreveport Martyrs continue to serve as a beacon of inspiration for generations yet to come, illuminating the path of sacrifice as a model for all. In honoring his life, we honor God, because we are reminded of the universal and accessible truth that our lives have their greatest meaning when we offer them for others.

Christophe Cardinal Pierre
Apostolic Nuncio to the United States
Washington, DC, October 1, 2024

ACKNOWLEDGEMENTS

This book is the third of a series, a follow-up to the book these authors published in 2021, *Shreveport Martyrs of 1873: The Surest Path to Heaven*. That publication chronicles the compelling story of five noble and heroic Roman Catholic priests who made a free offering of their lives during the 1873 yellow fever epidemic in Shreveport, Louisiana—the third worst that United States history records. Following shortly thereafter was a second book, *Shreveport Martyr Father Louis Gergaud: In His Own Words*. As an ongoing project rooted in friendship and reaching back several years, the research into the exemplary lives of all five priests (Father Isidore Quémerais, Father Jean Pierre, Father Jean Marie Biler, Father Louis Gergaud and Father François Le Vézouët) soon formed the basis of petitioning the Vatican's Congregation for the Causes of Saints for the necessary *nihil obstat*, that a canonization inquiry might begin. On December 8, 2020, Bishop Francis Malone of the Diocese of Shreveport acknowledged them as Servants of God. This marked the first step in what, hopefully, will be an ongoing cause for beatification and canonization that will extend beyond our own lives. The historical and theological work for the promotion of that cause continues and will, no doubt, for many years yet to come. Some of the biographical narrative about Father Jean Pierre, which proved to be foundational to both the previous book and the historical inquiry for sainthood, is therefore repeated herein. Not intended to be redundant, this vital information necessarily frames the context for his story across several works.

Through the process of ongoing research, we became aware of the existence of many of the personal letters of Father Jean Pierre, who at the time of his death from yellow fever on September 16, 1873, was serving as pastor of Holy Trinity Church in Shreveport. He built both the first and second churches, the second of which stood on the site of the current (third) structure. His selfless and tireless work endeared him to many, as evidenced in the abundance of secondary source material about him, and more importantly for our purposes here, his life is equally well chronicled in his own words.

Through original letters, which form a large portion of this manuscript, Father Pierre offers insights into significant historical scenes of local, regional and even national scope. He offers important commentary on the challenges of the northern Louisiana frontier of the mid-nineteenth century. His early days in Louisiana proved to be trying in many ways as he struggled with the language barrier, the weather and the customs of his newly adopted land, as well as the work that was ever before him. Yet the community of Shreveport and the surrounding mission areas deepened in their love and respect for the constancy of his presence among them. This is chronicled in many public documents and news reports. The most remarkable of these third-person accounts in the public record remember his free and willing offering of his own life in the horrific epidemic of 1873.

What emerges from the historical record is that a cult of devotion to Father Pierre began to develop immediately following his death. This is evidenced in the outpouring of public reaction and ongoing commemorations of his life and legacy. There is a sustained public record of remembrance of him, along with the other four Shreveport martyrs, across 150 years, to the time of this writing. He was a man driven to serve others, committed to the highest possible call, and even as a learned scholar and man of letters, he lived and walked humbly with those in need. This theme is punctuated by the clarity of his resolve to be the first to respond as a volunteer for the sick and dying in 1873. To this final task he turned without hesitation, knowing it would be his last mission in this life.

There are many people we wish to thank who made this project possible, including Bishop Francis Malone of the Diocese of Shreveport and the Chancery of the Diocese of Shreveport. Also, thanks to Bishop Robert Marshall of the Diocese of Alexandria. We wish to especially thank Bishop Denis Moutel of the Diocese of Saint Brieuc et Tréguier for opening the archives of his diocese and his hospitality. We also extend our ongoing gratitude to Christophe Cardinal Pierre, Apostolic Nuncio to the United

States, who has taken a great interest in all five priests, including Father Jean Pierre.

We are grateful to the University of Notre Dame Archives; the Archdiocese of New Orleans; Holy Trinity Catholic Church in Shreveport; the Diocese of Alexandria Archives in Alexandria, Louisiana; and the Noel Archives and Special Collections of Louisiana State University at Shreveport. These important historical depositories have diligently maintained the record that made this compilation possible. A special note of gratitude is reserved for the Louisiana State University at Shreveport Foundation, which has generously and enthusiastically supported the financial needs of ongoing research for this project, including the funding provided by the Hubert Humphreys Endowed Professorship in History, held by coauthor Dr. Cheryl White.

We offer a very special note of thanks to Audrey Garrett, who provided great assistance with the transcriptions and English translations of Father Pierre's original letters. The good priest's illustrative handwriting made this a challenging task at times, but Audrey's dedication to this project has had incalculable value. Our editor at The History Press, Joe Gartrell, has been a steady and patient guide through three successive book projects, for which we are most grateful.

Most of all, we thank Father Jean Pierre for leaving a legacy of his own words written across the pages of a selfless life and for leaving his indelible mark on the very identity of a city so torn apart by the ravages of deadly disease. The year 1873 marked a pivotal moment in the historical trajectory of Shreveport. After suffering so serious a population loss, the demise of the community itself might have seemed the most expected outcome. Devastated economically and challenged by the significant loss of a working class of people to rebuild what was lost, Shreveport nevertheless survived— and thrived—in the coming decades. Scholars can quite rightly attribute this renewal to factors such as new population patterns and emerging business opportunities, but these authors suggest that another contributor to the ongoing life of the region was something less measurable but perhaps even more significant. The presence of exemplary heroism, modeled in the life and death of Father Jean Pierre, provided a beacon of the best of humanity and doubtlessly attracted others to its light.

When the sad era, in the midst of which we now are, shall have passed away, and we have more leisure to devote to the merits of the dead, and more time to indulge our sympathies and tears, we trust that some worthier pen than our own, will do the life of Father Pierre, that high justice it so richly merits.
—Daily Shreveport Times, *September 18, 1873*

CHAPTER 1

THE FRONTIER MISSIONARY PRIEST

From Brittany, France, to Northwest Louisiana

In the picturesque medieval village of Lanloup in Brittany, France, Guillaume and Claudine Pierre welcomed a son into the world on September 29, 1831. The birth record lists only the given name Jean, and as a civil record, it of course offers little insight into family life or circumstances. Today, the tiny village of Lanloup with its few hundred residents still strongly echoes its medieval past, with only the occasional glimpse of modern influences on its ancient architectures and landscapes. One can observe this nowhere better than inside the fifteenth-century Church of Sant-Loup, where infant Jean was baptized the day after his birth. The medieval baptismal font still stands, having since witnessed countless more initiations into the Catholic faith.

It was this small rural farming village and its central community aspect of the church location that nurtured young Jean Pierre. The roots of Catholicism run deep in the history of this Breton culture, with documents dating its establishment to at least the early fourth century. The historical record is clearest by the fifth century, when bishops of the Brittany region were counted among those present at several notable synods, including the regionally important Council of Tours. This gathering in 461 met to discuss the "worldliness of the Gallic clergy." Among those known to be present were the bishop of Rennes, Athenius, and Mansuetus, identified as *"episcopus Brittanorum Armorica"* (today comprising the northernmost part of Brittany).[1] By the High Middle Ages, the region had witnessed a boom of church and abbey construction, with an organic spread of the faith

Above: Father Jean Pierre's birth certificate, Lanloup, Brittany, France. *Authors' collection.*

Opposite: The baptismal font in the fifteenth-century church of Lanloup, Brittany, France, where Father Jean Pierre would have been baptized. *Authors' collection.*

that cemented into the culture much of the uniquely Breton expressions of Christianity that continue today.

The fifteenth-century Church of Sant-Loup in Jean Pierre's small home village exemplifies the characteristic church-building style of the late Middle Ages, incorporating many of the distinctively Breton accoutrements. These included a typical parish walled enclosure of some type, with a surrounding cemetery often marked by a standing cross or Calvary depiction. This exterior depiction of the Passion was a deliberate aesthetic and architectural convention, meant to stand between the Church and the world, at the nexus of the living and the dead. The Church of Sant-Loup includes these notable features, currently maintained in their historical integrity.

It was as an ordinary child playing among these ancient stones and as a reverent altar server inside the church walls that young Jean Pierre first began to discern a call to the priesthood. The interior of the church contains significant artistic renderings that might have left important impressions on Pierre as a child, including some of its most prominent statuary. This region of Brittany witnessed several outbreaks of bubonic plague in the Middle Ages, and not surprisingly, churches dating to this era contained representations of the "Fourteen Holy Helpers," among them Saint Blaise and Saint Giles, as found in the Church of Sant-Loup. The connection between unpredictable pestilence, human suffering and the role of the Church in alleviating that suffering was visible and tangible in the very walls of the parish where Jean Pierre grew to young adulthood. The profound influence this imagery might have had on the young boy destined for missionary priesthood can only be surmised as significant indeed.

The pervasive and constant presence of death, obvious in every age, was perhaps no greater than in the Middle Ages, the precise period that produced the modern environs that the young Jean Pierre first came to know. Did he stand beneath the statuary images of the powerful intercessors, Saint Blaise and Saint Giles, and ponder their significance? Did he take

Above: The Church of Sant-Loup in Lanloup, Brittany, France, where Father Jean Pierre was baptized and served at the altar before leaving for seminary education. *Authors' collection.*

Opposite: Statue of Saint Giles at the church in Lanloup. Saint Giles is one of the "Fourteen Holy Helpers" often depicted in France, linked to intercessory devotion during various plagues throughout history. Father Pierre's exposure to such images and history undoubtedly had a profound influence on his spiritual formation. *Authors' collection.*

inspiration from hearing their stories? Did he first come to have a nascent understanding of sacrifice from their examples?

While little is known of Jean Pierre's childhood, he entered the Petit Seminaire de Tréguier on August 3, 1845, just weeks before his fourteenth birthday. He joined a student association known as the Congregation of the Most Holy Virgin, a community dedicated to the cultivation of deeper personal piety, with an added emphasis on assisting each other with scholastic excellence. This association required a formal written pledge, which Jean Pierre signed: "After satisfying a time of approval, Jean Pierre of Lanloup is received into the Congregation of the Most Holy Virgin established in the ecclesiastical school." It is an interesting observation noted in the school's own explanatory report that "most of the students who were members of this congregation later became priests."[2] This same Congregation of the Most Holy Virgin is, interestingly, noted in the formation of two of other Breton missionary priests who, with Father Jean Pierre, came to constitute the Shreveport Martyrs. Certainly the sense of brotherhood and shared identity in a higher calling and purpose did much to strengthen their resolve when their vocation demanded the supreme sacrifice of their own lives.

Institutional progress reports show that Jean Pierre was an exemplary student who excelled academically in every subject of his minor seminary studies. On October 1, 1852, Jean Pierre entered the Grand Seminaire de Saint-Brieuc. While from this point forward there is no surviving record of his progress in specific courses of study or further details of his academic capacity and piety, there is a signed document from the bishop of Saint-Brieuc, Jacques-Jean-Pierre Le Mée, which acknowledged Pierre's placement as second in his graduating class. Other primary records indicate that he received clerical tonsure on June 10, 1854, and departed for Natchitoches on October 8, 1854.[3]

The notation of "clerical tonsure" refers to an ancient sacred rite of the Catholic Church derived from the Latin word *tondere*, which is "to shear." It involves shearing of the hair as an outward sign of someone who is preparing for the reception of Holy Orders. While the tonsure is not, historically, an ordination, it represented an acknowledgement that Pierre was progressing in the discernment of his vocation as a priest. At the time that Jean Pierre was in seminary, the tonsure was widely practiced and therefore appears in his records, even on his entry to the United States.

In 1853, Pope Pius IX created a new diocese from within the Archdiocese of New Orleans that would cover much of the central and northern part of Louisiana. The Diocese of Natchitoches, erected on July 29, 1853, encompassed over twenty-two thousand square miles of territory, in an area of Louisiana that was only partially Catholic in religious culture or identification. Protestants had settled much of the northern part of Louisiana, engaged in either agricultural cultivation or commerce as the Red River became navigable in the first half of the nineteenth century. The community of Shreveport grew in response to the needs of an economically

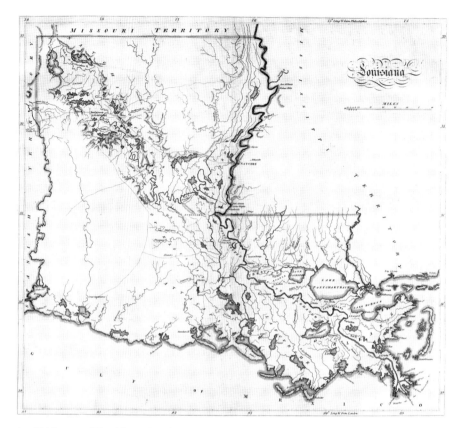

An 1845 map of Louisiana showing the area that became the Diocese of Natchitoches in 1853. *Library of Congress Prints and Photographs Collection.*

expanding nation, and the Catholic Church responded to this growth in direct parallel.

The first bishop of the new Diocese of Natchitoches was Auguste Marie Martin, himself a Breton missionary priest, originally from the seaport of Saint Malo. At the time of his elevation to the episcopate, Martin had been ministering in the United States for fourteen years. He knew well the challenges of his new diocese, including the most pressing one: recruiting enough priests to help spread the Catholic faith. To address this first urgent need, Bishop Martin traveled to Brittany to find young men willing to come to Louisiana.

In July 1854, Bishop Martin wrote to Archbishop Anthony Blanc in New Orleans that "the first and most important part of the mission in Europe has ended happily." He reported having found a sufficient number of young men willing to come to Louisiana, drawing principally from Saint Brieuc and Nantes. Martin also predicted that there would be other recruits through the "admirably generous" bishop of Rennes, at whose home Martin resided during his journey.[4] Indeed, the Diocese of Rennes would later yield yet another of the Shreveport Martyr priests of 1873, who would serve as assistant to Jean Pierre in Shreveport: Father Isidore Quémerais.

Jean Pierre was among the first group of Breton recruits that Bishop Martin brought to the new Diocese of Natchitoches. He received written approval from the Diocese of St. Brieuc to leave the diocese with Bishop Martin and embarked on a transatlantic journey that was the single most transformative event on his life's trajectory. The written record reveals that "upon the 21st October 1854, the Right Reverend Dr. Martin, Bishop of Natchitoches (United States) embarked at Havre, taking with him to his new diocese the following persons." The report continues to list, among many others, a simple entry: "Pierre, tonsured." This group included two others whose lives would also be inextricably linked to Jean Pierre's through the 1873 yellow fever epidemic of Shreveport: Father Louis Gergaud of Nantes, who was destined for Monroe, Louisiana, and "Levezouet, in Minor Orders, of Saint Brieuc," who was to become president of the seminary for the Diocese of Natchitoches.[5]

The young men arrived in New Orleans on December 5, the first Tuesday of Advent, after a forty-day ocean crossing. When they disembarked, they all would have heard the ominous news of another outbreak of yellow fever once again ravaging Louisiana. It was a portent of things to come.

Bishop Auguste Marie Martin, first bishop of the Diocese of Natchitoches. *University of Notre Dame Archives.*

This photograph of Father Jean Pierre is believed to date to the 1860s. The photographer is unknown. *Diocese of Alexandria Archives Collection.*

With unseasonably oppressive heat, the young recruits soon faced an uncharacteristically harsh drought. All of this was challenge enough, but this was also during the time they were trying to learn the English language, continue their studies for ordination and adjust to cultural differences. Father Jean Pierre confronted these challenges with what was to become a characteristic firm resolve, evidenced in his documented actions and writings.

With twelve young men now preparing for the priesthood in his new diocese, Bishop Martin appointed Father Pierre Dicharry vicar general and charged him with supervising their ongoing education and preparation in a small and informal seminary setting. Bishop Martin ordained Jean Pierre as a priest in Natchitoches, Louisiana, on September 22, 1855, just a week before Pierre's twenty-fourth birthday.[6] His first assignment was to build a parish church for a largely Catholic community, Bayou Pierre (named for eighteenth-century settler Pierre Laffitte, today this is Carmel, Louisiana, located thirty-three miles south of Shreveport in DeSoto Parish). A 1958 unpublished manuscript concerning the history of this region contains this observation: "How unusual to have a newly ordained priest appointed pastor immediately! Such was a sign of the great confidence that the bishop placed in the young Levite!"[7]

Bishop Martin probably had little choice but to trust the young Father Jean Pierre with such a mission. In the beginning, Martin had only a few priests to cover an expansive territory, and with the intention of growing the Catholic Church in the area, he addressed the most pressing needs of rural communities first—those that already had a small Catholic population. On the very afternoon of his ordination, Father Pierre learned he was not only to become pastor at Bayou Pierre but also to supervise the construction of a parish church.[8] In February 1856, Father Pierre purchased a plot of land from Joseph Laffitte for the sum of forty dollars, and the deed was registered to "the Right Reverend Bishop Martin and his successors for the use of a Church of the Roman Catholic Faith."[9]

Bishop Martin later noted the accomplishment: "Father J. Pierre has been appointed to a mission called Bayou Pierre. There he has bought forty acres of land and built an elegant church under the invocation of the Holy Apostles, Peter and Paul, and at the same time built a rectory for the priest."[10] However, secondary sources indicate that prior to the erection of the Diocese of Natchitoches, there had been a Catholic chapel somewhere near the Bayou Pierre community dating to the 1830s. It must haven fallen into disuse by 1853, as Bishop Martin clearly had no knowledge of such a structure existing.[11] It was during this time that Father Pierre's letters to

The Church of the Holy Apostles of St. Peter and St. Paul, which Father Pierre constructed in 1856 in Bayou Pierre, Louisiana. This was his first parish assignment. *Diocese of Shreveport Archives Collection.*

his bishop revealed much about the challenges that he faced. He frequently traveled to various mission areas, extending even to Shreveport, over thirty miles away. In 1856, after he finished the construction of the Church of the Holy Apostles, Father Pierre also established a small mission chapel in DeSoto Parish dedicated to Saint Ann and then turned his attention toward building a church in Shreveport.[12] Indeed, the missions in DeSoto Parish continued to grow and thrive following Father Pierre's initial contact there, as evidenced in his later correspondence and diocesan decisions about the need to build permanent churches.

Bishop Martin seemed concerned that Shreveport needed to be a priority, given its rapid population growth from the city's inception in the 1830s. In a letter to Archbishop Blanc in New Orleans dated April 3, 1856, Martin observed, "The important mission of Bayou Pierre is going well, but Shreveport is not yet provided for and how many more are still abandoned!"[13] Father Pierre's work in this isolated area of northwest Louisiana is all the more significant when viewed in its true historical context of an open mission field with little formal preexisting influence of the Catholic faith and where previous efforts to establish the faith had proved unsustainable. Writing again to Archbishop Blanc on February 25, 1857, Bishop Martin said he was sending Father Pierre to New Orleans to consult with him as "thus far, all efforts to establish in this town [Shreveport] whose commercial importance is growing, have failed…but Pierre will tell you how much good will he has found among Catholics, Protestants, and non-believers."[14] From its very beginning, the mission work of Father Pierre in northwest Louisiana bore much fruit.

Bayou Pierre, as Father Pierre's first mission field assignment in the Diocese of Natchitoches, has yielded a notable historical legacy. This same property continues to be owned and maintained by the Diocese of Shreveport. Some of its acreage became the site of a Carmelite monastery and school in 1891, which ceased to operate in 1904 following a series of fires that destroyed all structures but a small rock chapel. (Interestingly, it was the Catholic posture on racial equality that may have played a role in the demise of this institution. Secondary historical accounts suggest that two of the resident Carmelite monks were reportedly assaulted in acts of racially motivated violence.)[15] The State of Louisiana has designated this Catholic property a historical heritage site and placed a state marker there in 2020, noting the founding and lasting influence of Servant of God Father Jean Pierre, who "died a martyr to his charity in the Yellow Fever Epidemic of Shreveport in 1873."

Father Pierre, focusing his attention on the establishment of a church in Shreveport, was able to make considerable progress due to the generosity of local and regional Catholic families. Shreveport had been previously served by visiting priests who used public buildings, such as appears in this notice: "Our Catholic friends used the Court House October 26, 1854, which was Thursday, in the morning at 10 o'clock."[16] By the 1850s, the community's growth made it an undeniably urgent mission field for Catholicism. Its growth trajectory remains an interesting study for demographers, cemented in a unique narrative of United States expansionism and the economic boom following the Louisiana Purchase.

Shreveport, destined to be the epicenter of Father Pierre's heroic narrative, developed from purely economic needs in the early age of steamboats and rail. From New Orleans, cargo vessels increasingly turned northwest in the middle of the nineteenth century. In the summer of 1873, sustained steamer traffic churned its way up the Red River, though its channel was at times quite "narrow and snaggy."[17] The destination was Shreveport, along with a handful of her dependent towns in the river

Above: The Rock Chapel at Carmel, Louisiana (formerly Bayou Pierre). This chapel is all that remains of a Carmelite monastery built in 1891 on land purchased by Father Jean Pierre in 1855 for the construction of the Church of the Holy Apostles of St. Peter and St. Paul, acting on behalf of Bishop Auguste Martin. *Authors' collection.*

Left: Louisiana State Historical Marker commemorating the site of the Church of the Holy Apostles in Bayou Pierre. *Authors' collection.*

valley. Shreveport was emerging in the new decade as a busy port, rising from relative obscurity to become an important commercial waypoint on the road to the American West.

Perhaps even more than New Orleans, Shreveport existed for the reception and distribution of river-borne goods. Louisiana was the first state to enter the union after President Thomas Jefferson acquired the Louisiana Purchase territory in 1803. By the 1830s, Texas had become an independent republic, and speculators recognized the commercial opportunities of its neighboring Louisiana. In the upper stretches of the Red River, however, there was a significant challenge in the form of a logjam hindering navigation. Convinced

The logjam on the Red River in the nineteenth century known as the Raft. *State Library of Louisiana Collection.*

of the river's importance, the U.S. Congress appropriated funding for a remedy in 1828.[18]

In 1836, investors acquired land from the Caddo Nation and formed the Shreve Town Company, renamed Shreveport in 1839, bearing the surname of one of its founding members, Captain Henry Miller Shreve.[19] It was Shreve's work with the United States Army Corps of Engineers that had first cleared the "Great Raft." The rivercraft that Shreve chose to pass first through the Red River was the *Enterprise*, which certainly illustrates the ultimate objective of his work.[20]

At the time of his appointment, Captain Shreve was the superintendent of Western Waters, and lest his rank deceive, his previous service had been as a steamboat captain. Because Shreve held many patents on snag boats for debris removal and because he had successfully accomplished similar jobs before, he was a natural choice. Originally, the U.S. Army Corps of Engineers hoped to bypass the majority of the blockage by digging canals, but Shreve ultimately cut a fresh channel straight through it, forging a navigable river through American grit and determination.[21]

The completion of Shreve's project meant the northern portion of the Red River valley was open for business. Riverboats moved from New Orleans to the very doorstep of northeast Texas, a mere twenty miles from Shreveport, in just a matter of days. At the former trading post, purveyors laid out an ambitious sixty-four-block grid along the banks of the Red River.[22] The townscape was bounded on the north by Cross Bayou, on the east by the river itself, to the south by a backswamp generously called Silver Lake and to the west by a seemingly endless pine forest stretching to Texas.

Its growing and dense population, transient traffic, humid climate, stagnant water and abundant mosquitoes provided a recipe for the spread of a little-understood but often devastating disease: yellow fever. The first recorded outbreak in Shreveport in 1837 claimed the life of William Bennett, who was among the first permanent settlers. Nonetheless, optimism prevailed throughout the formative years, and as early as 1838, a correspondent with the *New Orleans Weekly Picayune* wrote:

> [Shreveport is] *a great thoroughfare for travelers to and from* [the Texas] *Republic....Light draught steamboats can reach the place all the year round....The town is improving fast. Eight new frame buildings are going up, including a large and spacious hotel. The settlers are remarkable for industry, intelligence and enterprise.*[23]

By 1850, Shreveport had a population of 1,700. Boardinghouses were hastily erected to accommodate the influx of people. In fact, many ordinary houses held nonfamily boarders, such was the shortage of residential accommodations.[24] Although land was plentiful, people were generally living in unusually dense proximity by American standards. The city attracted many immigrants, and the next decade saw a remarkable doubling of the population.[25]

Unlike in much of the agrarian South, in Shreveport, nearly a quarter of employed residents worked in commercial enterprise, including cotton brokers, grocery clerks, retail merchants and hardware store owners.[26] Commercial entrepreneurs made their presence known, and by the time of the Civil War, Shreveport exhibited a uniqueness "eminently cosmopolitan in…character, being made up of people from every state in the Union and from all nations of Europe."[27]

Although some areas were topographically well suited for efficient drainage, a city grading project begun in the 1850s remained half completed for want of funds and effective municipal leadership. In many localities, the natural drainage of the high areas toward the river, Cross Bayou and Silver Lake was diverted and leveled, without the requisite drains added. The result was that "a rain of a few hours convert[ed] the town into a morass."[28]

It was in this young city of Shreveport, in these specific economic and social conditions as starkly documented in the historical record, that Father Pierre began construction on the first Holy Trinity Church. This first church was but a small and basic wood-frame structure erected in late 1856 (the current structure, built in 1896, is the third iteration). Correspondence between Father Pierre and Bishop Martin throughout this time serves as excellent documentation of the progress of Pierre's mission work and his zeal for his ministry among the people of northern Louisiana. Father Pierre continued to serve the people of the Bayou Pierre community as well throughout this period, until Bishop Martin appointed the newly ordained Father Thomas Rebours to serve at Holy Apostles. However, Father Pierre formally maintained the title of pastor of Holy Apostles until 1858.[29] The distance between Shreveport and Bayou Pierre, more than thirty miles, was not an easy one, and travel certainly consumed a great deal of Father Pierre's energy and time as he continued to serve other small mission stations throughout DeSoto parish.

Surviving maps of the region are few, but those that do exist show few passable roads across the miles of distance that separated communities. A Confederate defense map drawn in the 1860s that depicts the Bayou Pierre community (a map that, importantly, documents the site of the Church of the Holy Apostles) shows one main road connecting the community of Bayou Pierre to others in the area. Road construction of the time was more intended for immediate purposes than predictable passability in all seasons, and the red clay of the region doubtlessly rendered these roadways difficult to traverse in wet weather conditions.

Therefore, with stifling Louisiana summer heat occasionally offset by heavy rains in the spring and fall, travel was among the foremost challenges that the young priest faced in these early days of his ministry. Nevertheless, Father Pierre rose to the challenges before him, as documented in the historical record. Bishop Martin praised Father Pierre to Archbishop Blanc in an undated letter, presumably from 1856 or 1857, in which he describes Father Pierre's episcopal visits throughout the northwest Louisiana missions, noting that the mission of Bayou Pierre was flourishing as a "jewel that does honor to Father Jean Pierre." In that same correspondence, Bishop Martin describes the plot of land acquired in Shreveport as being "in the center of town for $900, with $300 paid and the rest assigned to me."[30]

When the Diocese of Natchitoches acquired the land in Shreveport for the construction of a church, the location was accurately described as being "in the center of town." The city's original grid layout was sixty-four square blocks, with eight streets running west from the Red River and eight running south from Cross Bayou.[31] The city founders named streets with the intention of honoring many of the heroes of the Texas Republic, whose history is strongly connected to the earliest beginnings of Shreveport identity. The original property site that the Diocese of Natchitoches purchased in Shreveport was therefore intersected by the street named Milam. This name commemorated Benjamin Rush Milam, known for leading and falling in action at the Siege of Bexar in the fight for Texas independence in 1835. The next parallel original street was Travis, named for William Barret "Buck" Travis, who commanded the ill-fated Texian Army that made a famous last stand at the Alamo Mission in San Antonio in 1836.[32] The choice of property at this location, which already carried such weighted recognition in the identity of early Shreveport, secured a prominent place in the central business district for a major and highly visible Catholic building project.[33] The new church was also located within recognizable distance of longer-established religious entities in the city, including the Jewish synagogue and the Methodist and Baptist churches.

When he came to Shreveport, Father Pierre was able to quickly raise the rest of the funds for construction of the new church, offering his services as a private tutor for many of the local Protestant and Jewish families. The first Holy Trinity Church, built on the corner of Milam and McNeil Streets in Shreveport, was in operation by February 15, 1857, which is when the first baptism was recorded.[34] No photographs of this first structure are known to exist. By 1859, Father Pierre was supervising the construction of the second Holy Trinity Church, this one at the corner of Fannin and Marshall Streets (the site of the third and current church, which was constructed in 1896).

By this time, the diocese had also welcomed a group of ten Daughters of the Cross from Tréguier, France, of the Diocese of Saint Brieuc et Tréguier. This group was led by Mother Mary Hyacinth Le Conniat. They arrived in New Orleans in 1855 to meet with Bishop Martin and Archbishop Blanc. On the encouragement of Father Jean Pierre, the Daughters would go on to establish a new convent and novitiate in 1866 on the site of the old Fairfield Plantation, three miles south of Shreveport. This development set in motion a sharing of ministry between clergy and religious sisters that proved to be quite fateful.

Above: Drawing of the second Holy Trinity Church in Shreveport. *Diocese of Shreveport Archives Collection.*

Right: Mother Mary Hyacinth, Superior of the Daughters of the Cross in Shreveport at the time of the 1873 yellow fever epidemic. *Noel Archives and Special Collections, Louisiana State University at Shreveport.*

The establishment of the community of the Daughters of the Cross in Shreveport was fraught with some challenges as well, notably some disagreement between Father Pierre and his bishop about how best to proceed. The Civil War brought more than its expected share of economic loss to Bishop Martin's diocese, to say nothing of the effects of food and medicine shortages on the civilian population. Bishop Martin decided another return to France was necessary to present the Society of the Propagation of the Faith with a report of his needs, as well as to recruit additional missionaries from Brittany.[35] In his absence, Father Pierre acted to secure the purchase of property at a price and in a location he believed to represent a good use of resources for the future of Catholic education in the city. Bishop Martin initially responded to learning of the purchase with a sharp rebuke of Father Pierre's actions but later certainly assented that Father Pierre had acted prudently to secure low property prices in the immediate aftermath of the Civil War. The old site of Fairfield Plantation, two miles south of the central business district of Shreveport, became the site of Saint Vincent's Academy. Today, the site is the home of the offices of the Diocese of Shreveport.

The relationship between Father Pierre and Mother Hyacinth for promoting Catholic education actually preceded Father Pierre's formal ministry in Louisiana. While still in their native France in 1854, Father Pierre first approached Mother Hyacinth about the possibility of educating his own niece. He also mentioned that he would soon join Bishop Auguste Martin to begin missionary work in Louisiana. Mother Mary Hyacinth was instantly intrigued. Eventually, the bishop approved her and nine other Daughters to institute Louisiana missions. Throughout the 1850s and '60s, the sisters established chapter houses in New Orleans and Alexandria, Louisiana.

The first Catholic school in Shreveport dated to November 30, 1860, when Sister Theresa of Jesus and two other Daughters of the Cross came from Presentation Convent in Avoyelles Parish to establish Saint Mary's Convent. Father Pierre purchased property near Holy Trinity for that purpose. The enrollment response the first year required the construction of a second building in 1861. The outbreak of the Civil War meant a corresponding decline in enrollment, but this was the core of what later became Saint Vincent's Academy for Girls in Fairfield. Father Pierre's role in sharing a vision of Catholic education with the Daughters of the Cross marks a pivotal passage in the history of the entire region.

As rigorous as his view was of the need for Catholic education, as a pastor, Father Pierre was equally strict in his expectations of the public conduct and piety of the faithful. An example of this can be found in a letter of August 2, 1858, to Bishop Martin, appearing in its entirety elsewhere in this manuscript:

> *It has now been a month since I have preached Mass in Shreveport every Sunday. I have always had a large congregation there, and I have not had much to complain about in terms of behavior, except once. Eight days ago yesterday, there was a lot of noise; some laughed loudly, others chatted. As I am not in a mood to put up with such a thing, I scolded them quite severely, and I noticed that the children's newspaper, the* Junior Caddo Gazette, *mentioned this in my favor. Yesterday, whatever the cause was, nothing unprecedented, yet there were more people than last Sunday! The priest's position here requires great caution and tact; if he gives a little break, they will take advantage of it, if he scolds too often, he will make them resentful and lose interest in his warnings.*[36]

However, the strain of being a sole missionary priest occasionally wore on Father Pierre, who wrote in 1858: "I have endured a series of difficult days which will end in God's time. This state makes me unable to fulfill my duties and satisfy my requirements. I am going through a mental and physical prostration."[37] Despite the fatigue and rigorous demands of the mission field, Father Pierre persisted. Although a dramatic example of his malaise is found in this 1858 letter, further evidence reveals Father Pierre's profound level of commitment, renewed energy and excitement about the prospects of growing the Catholic Church in northwest Louisiana. This zeal is one of the attributes most often noted by independent historical observers.

Besides his public remembrance as a pastor, tutor and teacher, a long-lasting legacy of Father Pierre in Shreveport was his creation of the first public library. In 1868, the following public notice appeared:

> *Rev. J. Pierre requests a subscription list be open to establish a Catholic library, but one of general, useful, and varied information in the city of Shreveport....All will have access to the library on payment of a very small sum into its treasury, five cents for keeping for two weeks a volume under two hundred pages; ten cents for all larger books....The library will be open every Sunday morning after the High Mass....The money collected will created a fund, deposited with the treasurer, to buy new books and to subscribe to some good periodicals.*[38]

This library operated in Shreveport long after Father Pierre's death. It finally ceased to operate in January 1922, and until the end, it remained attached to his name and legacy. His commitment to literacy and learning promoted the substantial growth of an educated class in Shreveport, whom Father Pierre knew would be dependent on access to periodicals and classical works.

Because of his visible presence among the people and his commitment to ecumenical relations and outreach through literacy, Father Pierre became a recognizable public figure, associated with leadership. Although the city of Shreveport's Christian population was overwhelmingly Protestant (with a significant Jewish population noted as well), the people came to greatly admire and respect Father Pierre for his generosity, kindness and intellect. There are also many accounts of his care for the orphans and the poor, many of which are found among posthumous honors that appear in secular media reports of Father Pierre's death.

The success of his work among the people meant an expansion of the faith across the areas of northern Louisiana he served from 1856 to 1873. Father Pierre's labors in Shreveport were occasionally relieved by visiting priests, as noted in the sacramental registers of Holy Trinity. Yet it was not until early 1873 that he received the assignment of a permanent assistant priest: Father Isidore Quémerais. Working long hours, often isolated from brother priests and with little personal time away, Father Pierre came to embody the archetype of the nineteenth-century missionary priest.

Writing to the Propagation of the Faith in Paris in late 1872, in a letter giving his annual account of the Diocese of Natchitoches, Bishop Martin emphasized the often harsh conditions in which the priests, including Father Jean Pierre, found themselves laboring. They were engaged in a "fight against apathy in a small Catholic population, across a territory of a hundred leagues east to west, of a hundred and twenty north and south." Yet:

> *Year after year, infants were baptized, as they worked against the Voltairianism that dominated the comfortable classes, against the sensuality which was the only worship some knew…against the hatred of slaves and the poor classes, against the prejudice of Protestants which are three-quarters of the total population; against the Freemasons, always among us in this country.…I would have failed as a bishop without the conquering priests who have passed under my hands.*[39]

Father Jean Pierre photographed with an unidentified boy, likely an orphan in his care. *Diocese of Alexandria Archives Collection.*

Father Pierre's first sacramental registry entry at Holy Trinity Church in Shreveport. *Authors' collection.*

The sacramental registers of Holy Trinity Church and the records of the mission areas of DeSoto Parish provide prima facie evidence of the growth of Catholicism in northwest Louisiana during Father Pierre's tenure, even during the turbulent era of the Civil War.

Holy Trinity Church was large enough to warrant an assistant priest by 1872, and the independent historical record confirms that Father Pierre's role within the Shreveport community was a respected and admired one. It is not surprising that, with characteristic zeal and compassion, Father Jean Pierre would be among the first group of volunteers to organize medical and supportive care response in Shreveport when an epidemic of yellow fever broke out in late August 1873.

It proved to be his final but ultimate call to service.

CHAPTER 2

IN HIS OWN WORDS

Letters on Mission

Several original letters of Father Jean Pierre have survived, some of which are undated and are therefore placed in the presumed best historical context as follows here. The surviving correspondence with Bishop Auguste Martin spans the years 1858 to 1869, supplemented by some of the known correspondence from Bishop Martin in the years that followed. Within the lines of personal letters that he likely never imagined would be seen or scrutinized by the eyes of the future, Father Pierre offers the reader stark honesty. His insights into the conditions of northwest Louisiana, including both rural missions and within Shreveport, come from his unique perspective as one who often saw what others did not, frequently informed by his objective external view as one who did not know the area.

Each of the letters in some way touches on Father Pierre's mission efforts as a new priest struggling with language, culture and the harsh Louisiana climate conditions up to the period of the Civil War and its aftermath in the Reconstruction era. Most importantly, the letters shine great light on the strength of his personality, his serious nature, his occasional bouts of melancholy restored by hope, the personal struggles he overcame in his resolve to serve others and his immovable dedication to the mission of the Church.

Although his letters do not touch directly on the yellow fever epidemic of 1873, at least one missive, written fifteen years before the epidemic, keenly foreshadows what Father Pierre's resolve would be in that specific situation when it came to making a personal decision. The letters all provide important context for understanding the heart and mind of a priest who ultimately offered his own life within the mission field he nurtured. The majority of his letters follow in their full form, redacted only when necessary because of illegibility or lack of clarity. Most of Bishop Martin's responses are not known to have survived archivally, although some are referenced in secondary accounts. In many cases, the reader can only surmise Bishop Martin's response from follow-up correspondence. A comprehensive editorial note to apply to this correspondence: in this era, "Mr." was often used to refer to a priest, so the designation "Mr. Father" was not uncommon, as it appears with some frequency herein.

ON CHRISTMAS DAY 1857, Father Pierre took time to pen a lengthy letter to his bishop, updating him on the progress of the construction of Holy Trinity Church in Shreveport. Besides underscoring the urgency of building a church in Shreveport and providing updates on the status of financial affairs, the letter includes brief but interesting social commentary on the stigma attached to live theater performances that persisted into the nineteenth century. Father Pierre was insistent in informing his bishop that the taking of funds from a theater performance to apply to outstanding debt on the church's construction was not of his design, nor did he attend the event. This early letter establishes the tone that would become standard in future correspondence. Father Pierre wrote in a straightforward, serious and concise style, as evident in his account of the status of funding for the church. Within the letter, he makes a cursory but clear defense of having taken money from a theatrical performance, although one might be challenged to find such a thing scandalous today.

SHREVEPORT, DECEMBER 25, 1857

Your Excellency,

The walls of the Catholic Church of Shreveport are complete, and we have at last the pleasure and happiness of seeing what Shreveport has never offered before, a place where in the near future, Catholics will be able to come to worship God together. I do not yet know for sure what this part of the work will cost, since the bad weather prevented us from measuring the walls and paying off our expenses. I will not be able to pay *for the entire work, but I am assured of fulfilling the commitment made with the contractor. So far everything has been paid, in advance, and on the final arrangement that I have to make, I have already a deposit of $580. So he has nothing to complain about; I paid off his debts, I paid in advance, so I believe that he has every reason to be happy with me. As far as I am concerned, I am happy with him. The Catholic church will be and is already undoubtedly the most beautiful church in Shreveport. I look at it with pleasure, and I hope, Your Excellency, that you will also be satisfied with it. I do not want to anticipate anything; I would like for you to judge for yourself. If I were to give a more detailed description of it, I would be too impartial. I would see only beauty where a less forgiving eye would find flaws.*

Our God has blessed us far beyond our merits; despite the refusal of some members to pay, we collected fairly well and often in places where we had little reason to hope for relief. Therefore, the theatre company that came to Shreveport gave us the benefit of an evening's show, which earned $44. I would like for Your Excellency to notice regarding this offering that I did not ask for it and that no Catholic, at least to my knowledge, has taken part to obtain it. It is a Protestant, the husband of a Catholic lady, however, who I believe of his own initiative asked for a benefit for us. I am in great need of money, but I do not know if I would go to a theatre director to obtain it. Finally, whatever happens, I will accept the money, and I will even thank the director, who was said to have been charmingly polite in all his conduct in this affair. He wanted to let us choose the play to perform and to perform it on the day we wanted. A supper was also given for the church. It was, I was told, splendid. I did not attend it. Many people contributed to it, and we collected $110. So in the same evening, we made $150 thanks to these two events.

However, despite this help, we are far from having enough money to pay for everything. I therefore hope, Your Excellency, that you will come to our aid as liberally as you can. I believe, Your Excellency, that the church will be absolutely complete in February, and we would be happy if you would come and visit us at the beginning of May, next year, to consecrate the church and administer Confirmation to those who are willing.

We have a very pressing need for a church here, soon I will no longer know where to say Mass on Sundays and I would not be surprised to find myself obliged to suspend all ministry for lack of a suitable house. What a sad perspective for the heart of a priest, especially a priest in my position. Ah, I greatly need to say Mass, to eat the bread of the Strong, to triumph over the many difficulties that I encounter. Not everything in life can be rosy, and even the beautiful roses also have their thorns. So you see, Your Excellency, that I do need spiritual and temporal assistance. I hope you will most be kind enough to remember both. I am honored to be your humble servant,

J. Pierre, Priest

In April 1858, in what survives as a partial letter only, Father Pierre alludes to severe flooding in the city of Shreveport and the surrounding areas, something that is substantiated in the historical record. The spring season often brings heavy rains to the area, and in 1858, the rain levels were especially high, as referenced in several secondary source accounts. Indeed, Father Pierre's letter affirms as true what has been reported secondarily. The opening line refers to a person whose name is illegible. In context, Father Pierre seems to be referring to a contractor, perhaps for fulfilling some need for the new Holy Trinity Church. In the letter of May 1, 1858, that immediately follows, Father Pierre seems relieved to hear good news from Bishop Martin about the support of benefactors. This offers significant insight into the financial challenges that initially accompanied the establishment of a new church in Shreveport and, furthermore, offers corroborative dating of its first Mass.

Shreveport, April 24, 1858

Your Excellency,

Mr. ___ [possibly a contractor], *to whom your note was addressed, does not want or cannot even accept your conditions and therefore puts me in the most critical position I have been in. Cash alone, delivered on May 1, will satisfy his requirements, he says. I do not have any money right now, and I cannot raise any funds. They do not have any in the city, they say, or maybe they do not want to give me any, and the high water is preventing me from going elsewhere. I have already tried different means to get me out of this difficult situation, and none have succeeded.*

Fr. J. Pierre

SHREVEPORT, MAY 1, 1858

Your Excellency,

Your letter has relieved my heart from such heaviness! It came at the right time and relieved me from all my worries. I was on my way to visit my creditor when the good news arrived, and my fearful steps were strengthened by hope. Tomorrow, for the first time, I will preach at Mass at the church. We will pray for the benefactors, and please be aware that your beloved and revered name will not be forgotten. I have been sick in body and heart since our last visit in Natchitoches but am feeling quite well currently in both respects. I am going to come visit you.

J. Pierre, Priest

The following letter of August 2, 1858, speaks to the rapid growth of Holy Trinity Church in Shreveport and offers some interesting and even humorous insights into Father Pierre's rigid expectations of proper and pious conduct. His humility is subtle but genuine in his observations, which often minimize his own abilities and intellect—something that is clearly in contrast with what the local community remembered and honored about Father Pierre after his death in 1873. For further historical context, herein Father Pierre references Father Malassagne, who was among those Breton seminarians who embarked from the port of LeHavre with Bishop Martin and Father Pierre in October 1854 and was serving in Avoyelles Parish at the time of this letter's writing.[40] By this time, having established a church in Shreveport as both his bishop and his conscience led him to do, Father Pierre poignantly remained pastorally concerned about the welfare of those in the Bayour Pierre community left without a permanent priest because of his move.

SHREVEPORT, AUGUST 2, 1858

Your Excellency,

I do hope you will keep the promise you made to Mr. Malassagne to spend his holiday break at Bayou Pierre. The sooner he gets there, the better it will be for these good people, who have been deprived of a priest and exposed to death without the help of religion. I also have no doubt that Mr. Malassagne will come there with all the strength he needs to fruitfully exercise the ministry. When I came to Shreveport, there were sick people in *the area, and although they were not in danger, their condition may have worsened since then. It would therefore be good to hope that the priest who comes for a fairly considerable period of time among them may be as useful as possible. According to commitments made in Shreveport, I offer Mass every Sunday, and I will only be able to come for short visits to Bayou Pierre. I will be there on August 16 and 17 and will wait for or host Mr. Malassagne, and on the 19th or at the most the 20th, I will have to go back to Shreveport.*

It has now been a month since I have preached Mass in Shreveport every Sunday. I have always had a large congregation there, and I have not had much to complain about in terms of behavior except once. Eight days ago yesterday, there was a lot of noise: some laughed loudly, others chatted. As I am not in a mood to put up with such a thing, I scolded them quite severely, and I noticed that the children's newspaper, Junior Caddo Gazette, *mentioned this in my favor. Yesterday, whatever the cause was, nothing unprecedented, yet there were more people than last Sunday! The priest's position here requires great caution and tact; if he gives a little break, they will take advantage of it. If he scolds too often, he will make them resentful and lose interest in his warnings.*

Next Sunday, I am going to start a catechism and hold it every Sunday at 5:30 p.m. There will be Vespers; I invited little ones and adults, younger and older ones. I will do my best to make it interesting; it is the most effective way that I see for those who have never learned their duties and religion, or for those who have forgotten them.

A holy priest, eloquent speaker in English and scholar would do much good here. With someone who could captivate their audience with their delightful speeches, the church would soon be too small, and it would be necessary to extend it or build another one. I told you, Your Excellency, that I was going to be staying in Shreveport during the heat period, but I could not hold on. I have since visited Bayou Pierre twice…Homer and Minden once. These poor missions would need more frequent visits than I can fulfill; it is getting sad in some places.

My mission and I need Your Excellency, your good prayers; yes, we greatly need them.

Your Excellency, I am honored to be your humble servant.

J. Pierre, Priest

The following letter reveals the physical demands and spiritual challenges that befell Father Pierre as a frontier missionary priest attempting to cover vast amounts of territory with obviously limited resources. Writing in the summer of 1858, Father Pierre refers to a prolonged physical illness with symptoms that could be those of any viral illness but certainly align with yellow fever, especially given its summer occurrence. His chronic fatigue doubtlessly influenced the desperate tone of this letter to Bishop Martin, in which he submits himself for the bishop's judgement regarding whether or not to remove him from his duties in Shreveport.

SHREVEPORT, AUGUST 14, 1858

Your Excellency,

My health, which has been so good since I came back from Avoyelles, has considerably worsened for the last four or five days as I have been sick again. I had fever two or three times and also some chills sometimes. I have therefore begun a series of difficult days that will end in God's time. This state makes me unable to fulfill my duties and satisfy my requirements. I am going through a mental and physical prostration. It seems to me that I would need to spend a year or two in a position where the responsibility was less important and the physical fatigue less frequent. I have always been in places where I could say to myself: If I preach, these poor people will be able to educate themselves. If I do not preach, no one else will. If I fulfill this mission, the people will have the opportunity to receive the sacraments. If I neglect it, no one will replace me. When a man has to have such reasoning for Catholics spread over different parishes that include DeSoto, Caddo, Bossier, Claiborne and Bienville, the least enthusiastic man finds an irresistible motivation, he gets carried away and his health soon deteriorates from the fatigue of responsibility. If you therefore want me still to be able in the future to bear such fatigue and carry out missionary work, I believe the only way is to give me, for a little while, a position where there is less to do, or less spiritual and physical hassle.

You will perhaps tell me that now is not the time for me to leave Shreveport because of the debts weighing on our Church. Every single day, I do my best to ensure I have the necessary resources to finish paying them back, and I would not be at all surprised if someone else could not now succeed better than me. Well, he would do his best, but with your permission, I could still collect more money to help him. I am presenting with confidence, Your Excellency, my position, and I surrender myself just like a child surrenders himself to his father. Your wisdom will be crucial in your decision, and your care will lead you in determining what is best for the people and for their priest.

I am honored, Your Excellency, to be your very humble servant.

J. Pierre

The next letter in the surviving order, dated two weeks after the letter of August 14, contextually affirms the response that Father Pierre must have received from Bishop Martin offering a time to rest in Natchitoches, most assuredly in response to Pierre's physical and mental exhaustion. It also contains a reference to reports of yellow fever cases in Shreveport that summer that were in dispute among doctors. Eerily foreshadowing the great epidemic of 1873, Father Pierre offers an early insight into his charity and compassion for the people as he expresses concern that those infected could die without the sacraments, resolving to stay in the area despite the bishop's offer of a respite in Natchitoches. At a time of great physical fatigue, he turned down an offer to rest in order to stay among the people of Shreveport, for whom he clearly had pastoral concern and dedication. Interestingly, Father Pierre also cites among his reasons for remaining in Shreveport his concern about Protestant factions in the area having the potential to erode the Catholic population base that his mission work was seeking to sustain. Protective, pastoral and proactive: Father Pierre reveals all these aspects of his complex personality in the words of the letter that follows.

SHREVEPORT, AUGUST 28, 1858

Your Excellency,

I received today your kind and good letter of August 20, and I hasten to write you back. If you are fine with it, I will not accept your offer made to me to spend some time in Natchitoches for these three reasons which seem good to me:

1. The Protestants in Shreveport are making extraordinary efforts to strengthen their faltering religion and to cause defection among the Catholics. There were protracted meetings in Shreveport; there are some in Keatchie; there is a "camp meeting" at Pleasant Hill; there is another in Texas not far from the border, where the preachers are making considerable efforts to corrupt the Catholics. One young man already has become a Methodist, and another one, I heard, has become a Baptist. My leaving in such circumstances would perhaps be a reason for others to leave the Church as well. The presence of the priest, the Mass, the prayers to which he calls the faithful are, I believe, powerful means of resistance to being drawn into this evil.

2. Last week, some doctors here believed that there were two cases of yellow fever, but the assertion was refuted by other doctors. In any case, we are afraid of the yellow fever coming, and I would fear that by leaving, Catholics could die without the sacraments, and that they could say the priest feared the disease and left because of it. Rather than giving an opportunity for someone to publicly accuse the Catholic priest, I would rather die twenty times on the battlefield. As of now, health remains very good overall in Shreveport.

3. I think that in Natchitoches, I will be in less favorable conditions than here to regain my strength and courage. I would worry about my poor congregation. I would fear seeing defections on my return. I would be concerned about abandoning them in the middle of danger, and all together, this would prevent me from enjoying a restful time in Natchitoches. I would only be relieved once I return, and it would, I believe, do more harm than good. Therefore, I desire not to leave.

I am honored to be your very humble and devoted servant,

J. Pierre

The following letter from October 1859 refers to the question of the establishment of the Daughters of the Cross in Shreveport, should Bishop Martin approve it. Father Pierre boldly asserts his opinion, concerned specifically about the lack of Catholic education in Shreveport. Father Pierre also asserts the lack of formal educational opportunities for the girls of Shreveport, displaying a pressing concern for this inequity.

SHREVEPORT, OCTOBER 3, 1859

Your Excellency,

Your Grace advises me, based on your last letter, to ask the Daughters of the Cross to come and settle in Shreveport; this request has already been made and at least listened to with pleasure; consent is still adjourned because of the great expenses that this move will cause and also because we do not know if Your Excellency will approve the project. Your Excellency notes that it will only be slowly that the sisters will be able to extend their work; this assertion does not seem to me to reconcile well with what I see:

in three years, these sisters founded three houses, which are doing quite well. It seems to me that this is a very fast development.

Your Excellency informs me that the sisters can barely support their buildings and this only by further compromising their health. I believe the Superior keeps an eye on these matters, and if I know her well, she is not a woman to put the health of her good daughters at great risk, so I leave this care to her decision.

Your Excellency wisely implies that I have to shake off the burden of debt which weighs on me before yielding under another one. I currently have $565 of debt, and let's suppose this debt rises to $600 by next year. If Your Excellency keeps the promise you made to help Shreveport, as I hope, by $400 or $500 more in 1860, I hope I can also pay the rest, so I am hopeful to be able to do something for the sisters, in one way or another.

Your Excellency believes that Shreveport, with its current population situation, is not in a position to offer its religious community a sufficient number of Catholic students to justify such a building. Is Alexandria any more so? I do not know. Does Your Excellency hope that Shreveport will be in the future, without any Catholic schools, a more pleasant place for my religious community? I believe the opposite, for this good reason: there is currently no public school in Shreveport for girls, nor any school worth the name. The first to be established will be supported for lack of anything better, if it is good. It deserves confidence, and it will be able to boldly defy all competition. Do you want the Protestants to have here again this advantage over us of having all the schools in their hands? Let a Protestant school be built in Natchitoches, and then create a Catholic competition; you will see how successful it will be, knowing that Natchitoches is predominantly Catholic. What would it be like in Shreveport? No one better than Your Excellency knows the importance of choosing the right moments and of not letting advantageous opportunities slip away, which often never come back.

Please therefore answer me if the sisters, agreeing to come to Shreveport and to take upon themselves the expenses of this foundation, will receive your approval, leaving them free to choose the time they deem suitable and to send how many and whoever they want.

I am honored to be Your Excellency's very humble servant,

J. Pierre

The next surviving letter dates to several years later, in 1868, after the conclusion of the Civil War. No known letters from Father Pierre in the intervening years survive, and this lapse in the record could be due to a variety of reasons. The inflationary cost of paper during the Civil War years made lengthy and frequent correspondence impractical, especially if the writer of the letter intended to maintain a copy of his own. Furthermore, the paper and ink products available during the war years may also have been created from inferior processes with resultant poor quality that negatively impacted document survivability during this period. It is possible that there may have been writings by Father Pierre that were lost or destroyed as a consequence of war.

Regardless of what he may have expressed to his bishop in the intervening years, the resumption of Father Pierre's primary record of letters in 1868 is consistent in its expression of concern for proper conduct and order, reflecting the familiar diligence and obedience found in his previous correspondence. On this occasion, the progress of Holy Trinity Church included the acquisition of a new bell but under less-than-ideal conditions. As in an earlier letter, the circumstances Father Pierre relates to his bishop as potentially scandalous might seem minor to the current culture but would have been of particular concern at the time. Therefore, contextually, the tone and urgency of this letter regarding "this unfortunate bell" reflects Father Pierre's sincere, conscientious concern that the Catholic presence in Shreveport be above any type of moral reproach. For appropriate and full historical context, it is helpful to remember that at the time of this writing, Father Pierre surely knew of the work of the Second Council of Baltimore (1866), which had just outlined:

> *We consider it to be our duty to warn our people against those amusements which may easily become to them an occasion of sin, and especially against those fashionable dances, which as at present carried on are fraught with the greatest dangers to morals.*[41]

SHREVEPORT, MAY 13, 1868

Your Excellency,

I have to submit to Your Excellency a serious case which embarrasses me greatly. To be explicit and well understood, I must start at the beginning. About a month ago, a Catholic from Shreveport gave me $240 to pay for a bell that weighs 1,000 pounds for the church. This bell was ordered from New York and is probably today on its way to Shreveport. The donor wants the bell to hang 100 feet high. The tower needed for this will cost money, and my congregation knows that I do not have any.

To meet this expense, two Catholic ladies thought of giving a ball. They came to propose their plan. I did not like it, and I told them so. However, they do much that they managed to get my agreement on it, provided that the ball was held without any of the dances forbidden by the Church—waltz, polka, etc.—and that I would be personally ignored in the event that I would be involved in anything, answering for nothing.

This evening the ball took place, and imagine my surprise to see the polka and the mazurka appearing on the program. Apparently the two ladies in question knew nothing about it either until around 6:00, an hour too late to remediate it. So how to fix it! The city's elite—lawyers, doctors, merchants, Protestants and Jews—got involved and took charge. There are less than a quarter of Catholics involved in planning.

Although this is to help the Catholic Church, it is not considered Catholic; rather, it is a means adopted by the city to achieve this goal. It even seems that my two Catholic ladies, who were the first driving forces, have repeatedly said that I did not approve of it and that I was by no means responsible.

However, it will always be true that if I had absolutely opposed it in principle, it would not have happened!

Now, Your Excellency, what to do!

The matter is serious, and I will not do or say anything on the subject until I receive your response. Should I accept the money and apply it to the donations? On the other hand, should I refuse it and give it in charity to the poor? I will deposit in the bank while awaiting your decision.

Should I blame the situation on others in public, in church, or in the newspapers? Or should I remain silent? Remember that the most influential non-Catholics of Shreveport were involved and that it is their affection either for the Church or for me that will have motivated them and that in their minds, a ball is a legitimate means to raise funds. I intend, if you approve, to tell the church here that never again will we hold a ball to help either the church or any Catholic business.

There is also not the slightest doubt that many Protestants and perhaps even Catholics will be scandalized or offended by the process and will say that it was resorting to very non-Christian means to obtain money and will blame both the church and myself for not having prevented such a thing.

I believe, Your Excellency, I have clearly explained the situation to you. Please be kind enough to give it your attention and tell me as soon as possible what I must do. This unfortunate bell has already bothered me *and threatens to be a heavy burden for me in the future. Your Excellency, however, can remain assured that I will not go into debt in these difficult times to have the pleasure of hearing it ring.*

It has been agreed with the donor that upon its arrival in Shreveport it will be housed in a store until we have the means to mount it, should it stay there for six or even twelve months.

Your humble and respectful servant,

J. Pierre

In July 1869, Father Pierre wrote to Bishop Martin to express concern about the conduct of a priest whose name was not legible or clearly identified who may have functioned as a chaplain for the Daughters of the Cross and against whom charges of drunkenness and poor public behavior had been made. Noting his own lack of direct observation in the matter, Father Pierre reserves judgement about the other priest but also points out that the care of Shreveport requires assistance. The growth of the parish of Holy Trinity is apparent from his concern, however, as he also describes the challenges of providing for the pastoral needs of the growing Catholic community. Importantly, Father Pierre again emphasizes his personal concern that the people of Shreveport be assured of access to the sacraments, explaining that a sole priest was insufficient for ensuring that no one died without receiving them.

Shreveport, July 26, 1869

Your Excellency,

It is very embarrassing for me to respond to the letter that Your Excellency has written to me. Does Your Excellency know if [name illegible] *drinks? Some people think so. I did not see him drunk and I even have much doubt that he was. With his lively personality, hot temper and animated conversation, along with his colorful face, it is easy to do him injustice in this respect. Many would take him for crude, when perhaps really he is not.*

Should his personality allow him to be left in his present position? I am not sufficiently aware of the relationship he has to be able to pronounce this an excess. I know there were mutual complaints. Your Excellency will realize that I do not dare to speak.

Your Excellency may see what position I will find myself in if I am left alone in Shreveport. I would be about 100 miles away from any fellow priest in the diocese. With my recurrent weak health, I would find myself alone in charge of a parish where there is much to do. If I do not preach two Masses each Sunday, many Catholics will miss hearing it, communions will be considerably reduced and I do not have as many yet as I could. I would have to take care of a boarding school, two and a half miles from the city, and one or two day schools, along with all the missions connected to Shreveport. If the number of Catholics in those missions is not considerable, the distance to visit them is.

This, in a few words, is the position of the priest in Shreveport if left alone. If he died, there is a 99 percent chance out of 100 that neither he nor his people would receive the last sacraments.

Because I have heard there is mutual dissatisfaction between the Sisters and their current chaplain, if there is a way to change him for another, things would improve.

May the good Lord inspire Your Excellency to decide everything for his glory. Your burden as bishop must weigh on you frequently. Your Excellency is in charge of a diocese where ministry is difficult; the priests are devoted, but most are broken and tired and old before their time. But, finally, let's take courage! Let us do all we can for the glory of God, and His blessing will rest upon us.

May Your Excellency bless me.

I am honored to be Your Excellency's very humble and respectful servant.

Father Pierre

By September 1869, the expansive growth of Catholicism in northern Louisiana has taken prominence in Father Pierre's reporting to Bishop Martin. The following letter includes great insights into the developing patterns according to specific regional geography, which is most helpful in framing and understanding not only the growth in religiosity but also demographics in this period of Louisiana history. Father Pierre speaks to the need for a church in the nearby community of Mansfield, a vision of his that indeed came to fruition.

Father Pierre also refers to the need for a chapel in Minden in Webster Parish and the growth of the Catholic community in Bellevue, the community that served as the first seat of Bossier Parish from 1843 to 1888. Interestingly, the reference herein to the community of Bellevue is especially noteworthy, since it was to that community that Father Pierre's assistant pastor at Holy Trinity, Father Isidore Quémerais, retreated to convalesce from tuberculosis before making a fateful return to Shreveport in September 1873 when yellow fever broke out. The Catholic community of Bellevue, so nurtured by Father Jean Pierre, not only provided a place of respite for his young assistant but also later proved to be among the towns unaffected by the epidemic. Therefore, when Father Pierre later summoned his Father Quémerais to return to Shreveport to assist, Father Quémerais left one of the most remote and, therefore, safest of environs to enter a city so infected with yellow fever that he would live less than two weeks. This letter provides important context for Bellevue having been an important and growing mission area.

This letter also contextualizes Bishop Martin's travel to the First Vatican Council as he leaves Father Pierre with responsibility during his absence. Father Pierre includes a reference to the opening of the "Day School in Shreveport."

From a sociological perspective, the following September 19 letter highlights what can only be seen as points of rivalry, if not conflict, between the historically strong Baptist presence in the region and the emerging Catholic presence. The relationship between these communities in northern Louisiana mirrored that found elsewhere, especially in the Deep South, marked by a complex array of differences in doctrinal and social teachings. These differences frequently led to tension and misunderstandings, evidenced by Father Pierre's commentary in the following letter, which no doubt hinged also on the settlement patterns of northern Louisiana. The nineteenth century in rural Louisiana generally reflected lower levels of the kind of educational attainment that might have informed greater understanding and tolerance. Catholicism, as the relative newcomer to this part of Louisiana in the mid-nineteenth century, was viewed with varying degrees of suspicion and also probably a good measure of curiosity, due to the prevailing social and religious attitudes that characterized early settlement.

SHREVEPORT, SEPTEMBER 19, 1869

Your Excellency,

I sincerely thank you for the trust Your Excellency gave me. I will do what I can to deserve it. I do not anticipate that the Sisters will have any important steps to take during your absence, other than to try, if possible, to have a chapel built in Fairfield. If I am not mistaken, Your Excellency recognized the necessity of having another place for Masses other than the very small room which is assigned there.

As the (temporary) chaplain, I plan to do for the Sisters what other pressing obligations and my health will allow me. The Day School in Shreveport opened last Wednesday with 20 students.

Our small boys' school also has 20 students, of which there are 15 Catholics. At a rate of $2 per month, assuming that everyone pays, which is far from certain, there will still be a deficit of $10 at least to make the $50 monthly minimum salary payment promised to Miss Craig. From a financial standpoint, our boys' school does not promise much, but things can also change for the better, and if even at this price we can do some good for the emerging generation, it is well worth it. The Protestants seem more united than ever against us in Shreveport; the Baptists especially want to win over all, hands down. They managed to poach two or three weak Catholics from me, and they still surround a few others in their network. The struggle will be strong for some time, but I like to believe that this storm, like several others that I have seen rising around us, with the Grace of the good Lord, will also dissipate entirely or at least diminish. These are human efforts which not having the grace to succeed, after having made noise and causing more or less harm, eventually cease.

I was told that the Baptist preacher on Sunday preached a sermon of which I was the main subject. I feel pity for him if he does not have a more important subject to discuss before his congregation. Perhaps eternal matters might have made a better topic.

From two or three different sources, I learned that there is a subscription list already amounting to 1,500 in Mansfield to build a Catholic church there. It is also said that many non-Catholics have the matter at heart and want to see the success of this venture as keenly as the few Catholics in the area. If this is true (at least there must be some truth to it), it would be good to place a priest in this poor DeSoto Parish.

I am told that it would be easy also to build a chapel in Minden, if there were a priest serving the Catholics scattered there and in Claiborne Parish. On my last visit, I baptized a Dr. McFarland, who it is said would happily give the land to build on. During my last visit to Bellevue, I baptized 5 or 6 children of Protestants, or should I say of non-Catholics, after the parents promised to raise them in our Holy Faith. One of them has since died, so for this one there is no doubt. At the cost of numerous sacrifices and continuous dedication, the priests in these places could, with the grace of the good Lord, do good. We must not forget that this would be imposing on them a difficult task for which good health, courage, perseverance and complete abnegation would be required. God sends us men of this caliber.

May God keep and protect Your Excellency. May Your Excellency provide Shreveport and its rector a blessing from the bottom of your fatherly heart.
I am honored to be Your Excellency's very humble and respectful servant.
Father Pierre

Here, the documented correspondence between Father Jean Pierre and his beloved Bishop Auguste Martin concludes. Although there are surviving letters from Bishop Martin that postdate this archival record, the preceding letters represent the known written record in Father Pierre's own words, with the exception of newspaper references that quote him and his last will and testament.

CHAPTER 3

WITH SELFLESS LOVE

Father Jean Pierre in the 1873 Yellow Fever Epidemic of Shreveport

The first warning of an impending crisis in Shreveport in the late summer and early fall of 1873 came insidiously, cloaked under the vague historical remembrances of previous fevers that had visited the river port. It is likely that most of the city scarcely noted the warning at first, precisely because the nature of previous outbreaks had been mostly mild, even though yellow fever had claimed the lives of distinguished city figures in the past. For instance, early settler and entrepreneur William Bennett succumbed to the illness in 1837, as did his business rival James Cane in 1845. The deaths of these two early pioneers testified to the dangers of a locale that offered the perfect storm for a large-scale epidemic, if it ever was to come: a dense human population concentrated on a riverfront with transient commercial traffic, a large mosquito population and, occasionally, rainy seasons that produced great amounts of standing water—in other words, the right conditions for a mosquito-borne illness to spread indiscriminately. Such was the case beginning in late August 1873.

The city was already known for its often unsanitary conditions as, even by this time, the public sewage system was incomplete. The "sewerage was so defective that the refuse of the hotels and boarding houses was [simply] poured out upon the surface of the ground" for easier disposal.[42]

> *As early as January [1873] the accumulated filth in the alleys of the city began to be oppressively offensive....Furthermore; the most public thourough-fares [sic] of the city were totally neglected; stagnant water,*

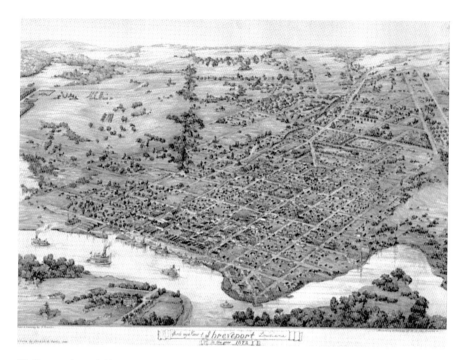

Bird's-eye view of Shreveport showing the Red River and settlement, 1872. *Authors' collection.*

rotten garbage, animal excrement, filled the gutters; the refuse of hotels and boarding houses in every portion of the city poured out of private sewers, into the streets, there with dead cats, dogs, and rats to fester and emit the most noisome stench.[43]

Adding to the perfect storm of accumulating circumstances, the summer of 1873 in Shreveport was a historically wet one, and the streets were "neglected and uncleaned; stagnant water, rotten garbage and animal excrement filled the gutters....The whole city [was] enveloped in a disgusting odor, from midnight to day."[44] "A sanitary police is unknown, and the only scavengers are hogs, which roam the streets at will, turning them into cess-pools."[45] Blame for the deplorable state of public health was routinely laid at the feet of the municipal government.[46]

Adding to the looming public health crisis was the fact that there was no public supply of suitable drinking water. Wells were not feasible so close to the waters of the Red River. The only reliable source of fresh water at the time was found at Currie's Spring, a considerable traveling distance from downtown.[47] Water purchased from this spring cost five cents per bucket, which kept the poor away. Instead, most collected rainwater in massive cypress and brick storage cisterns. Little did anyone know that this water, left standing for even a few days, became the prime breeding ground for the mosquito carriers of yellow fever.[48] The mosquito breeding cycle can vary from as few as four to fourteen days, depending on a variety of factors.

The great yellow fever epidemic poised to strike Shreveport in 1873 began when riverboat crewmen and other strangers made their way to the Market Street Infirmary at Market and Travis Streets, just two blocks from the riverfront and mere steps from Holy Trinity Church. There, in the medical offices of Drs. Darwin Thornton Fenner, Thomas G. Allen and William Henry Williams, three strangers were diagnosed with "remittent fever."[49] It was the high fever season, and although the town had already seen its share of yellow fever in its short history, most would have been unwilling to call this disease what it likely was. Even drawing from history, there was no exact precedent for what Shreveport was about to witness.[50]

The infirmary physicians recognized that an outbreak among the steamboat men would spread quickly, without knowing exactly why.[51] Further complicating the situation, several captains were taking advantage of the high water as they lined up their riverboats along the upper and lower landings on the Red River. Among the line of steamers waiting idle was the *Ruby*. The vessel was tied up south of town with crew making repairs and building cow pens while awaiting a load of cattle for the New Orleans market.[52] Despite the odor, Shreveport's dank streets were awash with inactive steamboat men and visitors celebrating the completion of the grand westward-reaching railroad, just recently accomplished. The age of the steamboat intersected the great age of rail transport, and the history of commerce in the United States was forever changed. Shreveport was a shining example of unprecedented progress.

In fact, earlier in the month, the *Daily Shreveport Times* carried lengthy editorials on the promising commercial future of Shreveport with the opening of the Texas & Pacific Railroad, predicting great crowds visiting for a celebration of such remarkable progress and appealing to the merchants to invite visitors into their stores—and even into their homes. Shreveport's hotels had filled quickly, and the city was abuzz with activity and excitement. Because of the river levels, shipments arrived and departed daily through the booming port. Certainly, no one wanted to dampen this enthusiasm.

Meanwhile, however, the tally of suspicious fever cases quickly and quietly rose, but the community found the troubling news was difficult to contain, as medical practitioners disagreed about the common denominator being yellow fever. To even suggest the illness was yellow fever was to threaten an absolute cessation of economic activity, and in a city so dependent on commerce, this represented an unpopular and damaging call for officials to make. Still, the horrible reality quickly became undeniable.

IN MID-AUGUST, CERTAINLY PUNCTUATED by the celebration of the Solemnity of the Assumption of the Blessed Virgin Mary on August 15, Father Jean Pierre and his assistant, the young Father Quémerais, were spending their days attending to routine parish life in the city's only Roman Catholic church. By 1873, the rolls of parishioners had grown with great vigor, as attested to in the sacramental history of the parish. Augmenting Father Pierre's ministry in the city by this time was the presence of Father Quémerais, although he was frequently unwell, with a history of what symptomatically presented as tuberculosis.[53] Father Quémerais had not been in Shreveport long, having just arrived the year before, but certainly had fond memories already of his time serving alongside Father Jean Pierre. His first baptism in Shreveport was dutifully recorded on Passion Sunday, March 30, that same year, in the Holy Trinity register—that of the infant Francis John Flanagan.

In the days of late August and early September 1873, it is difficult to separate the narrative of the two Holy Trinity priests. Although Father Pierre clearly emerged among the earliest of leaders in the relief efforts responding to the epidemic, Father Quémerais also made a choice to serve alongside his pastor, in lockstep, until the fate came that awaited them both.

The fates of the two Shreveport priests had been sealed together since Bishop Auguste Martin responded to Father Pierre's repeated requests for assistance in Shreveport. In addition, Catholics of Shreveport apparently had also noticed the demands on Father Pierre and his need for help. In a letter dated February 24, 1872, eighteen months before the yellow fever outbreak, Bishop Martin wrote at length to Father Pierre about the unique and pressing pastoral needs of Shreveport, informed by a variety of sources:

> *On yesterday, Friday, my very dear friend, I received your two letters, and on Monday last another letter of a previous date accompanied by several lines from Mother Le Conniat. I have answered all three, but only briefly, because I have some other letters to write tomorrow and also because I have to prepare my instructions....*
>
> *As to the Redemptorist Fathers, yes, I would desire them and would like for them to be in Shreveport so that there they might promote the welfare*

Father Isidore Quémerais, photographed in 1872 outside Holy Trinity Church in Shreveport. Father Quémerais served as the assistant to Father Pierre and died of yellow fever on September 15, 1873, just one day before Father Pierre.

of my diocese and the good of Texas. But does this help, as the Reverend Fathers do not at all want to administer a parish, and so even though they have consented to accept the work, nothing will be done until matters concerning this have been opened and handled with the consideration in view of the entire interior of the country, as well as after the advice of the Superior of this order's province has been obtained. In a word, when and where is the secret of Providence? The results are known to Providence only, as to when and where the Fathers will come to establish a foundation here. Let us await this time and act as though we expect nothing.

Regarding the vicar, the assistant priest: yes, you need one, and the sooner the better. This is one of my fondest hopes and desires. If his health would improve, Father Quémerais would be your man: devoted, kind, studious, zealous and already familiar with the English language. But, in truth, I fear that he would be a burden to you. I will see him a little after Easter. If I think he is in a state of health to help you, I will send him to you, even if only temporarily while waiting for someone else.

I will do all I can for you and for Shreveport. Please transmit this assurance to those of your Catholic flock who, in a letter to me dated the 18ᵀᴴ, made a similar request to me for an assistant pastor. We have only 22 priests, and we need 40. Therefore, ask the Lord to help me.

At Holy Trinity Church on Monday, September 1, 1873, the faithful marked the Memorial of Saint Giles, one of those "Fourteen Holy Helpers" known to Father Pierre from his formative childhood years at his family's parish church in Lanloup, France. Intersecting this memory for him would have been the brutal reality of summer's resurgence, with a rise in daily temperatures, and the stark certainty of a mounting death toll. The statistics to come would parallel anything that the tiny village of Lanloup had known during medieval plague outbreaks. Did Father Pierre make this connection on the day that he memorialized Saint Giles? He was likely too busy with the grim task of organization that he knew confronted him, as well as every other prominent leader of Shreveport. Yet still, his life as a priest continued, perhaps especially amid the gathering uncertainty.

It is therefore fitting to presume that on that centuries-old Feast of Saint Giles, as he celebrated Mass, Father Pierre was at least momentarily transported to his homeland, where he would have once stood before the statue of Saint Loup above the church's entrance.[54] The parish priest certainly had Pierre memorize the prayers *Ad Deum qui laetificat juventutem meam…* and the *Suscipiat Dominus* and all the postures and gestures, as altar boys had done for centuries. In turn, this is what Father Pierre taught to young altar servers in his adopted home of Shreveport at Holy Trinity Church.

There can be no question that with his keen skill, intellect and memory, Father Pierre would have at least fleetingly recalled the saints depicted in glass and statuary. While looking at the likenesses of Saint Giles and of Saint Blaise, he learned to pray to them for protection against plagues. Saint Blaise was the special patron of diseases of the throat, and Father Pierre held the memory of having newly blessed candles placed at his own throat every February.[55]

Father Pierre knew their stories and had assimilated them into his own life of priestly ministry. Their exemplary lives inspired: Bishop Blaise, in Sebaste, Armenia, in the year 316, imprisoned for refusing to renounce his faith, miraculously saved a young boy from choking on a fishbone, although that alone did not convince the governor to be merciful. They beat the saintly bishop and then ripped his flesh with iron combs before ultimately beheading him.

The statue of Saint Giles also held a prime location on the high altar in Lanloup, so that at every Mass, the young Jean Pierre must have gazed upon him. "Sant Gilles" was one of the most popular saints of France and Germany. This seventh-century Athenian performed miracles but longed for a life of solitude and chose to live in a cave in France. Tradition holds that a God-sent deer nourished him with her milk. A hunter's arrow meant for the deer hit the saintly hermit, to the remorse of the hunter, who turned out to be the local king. Saint Giles refused the king's physician and compensation but instead asked the king to build a monastery. He agreed, on the condition that Giles serve as its abbot. The arrow wound made Saint Giles the patron of those with disabilities, specifically invoked for protection against plague.[56] Saint Giles died peacefully around 720, not a martyr but, as the word *martyr* means, a true witness to the faith.

In Shreveport in early September 1873, on the leading edge of an epidemic that was to claim his own life, it was certainly these traditions that shaped the living faith of Father Jean Pierre. Before he entered the meeting rooms of other citizens to decide the course of action to deliver compassionate care and relief to the city, it was this faith that strengthened him, as on that day, Father Pierre continued the *Os iusti* Mass, the Mass for a sainted monk, for protection from diseases, that the people be spared the devastation experienced in fourteenth-century Europe. He proclaimed aloud the Gospel passage from Saint Matthew on that day:

Then Peter said to Jesus in reply, "We have given up everything and followed you. What will there be for us?" Jesus said to them…"Everyone who has given up houses or brothers or sisters or father or mother or children or lands for the sake of my name will receive a hundred times more, and will inherit eternal life.[57]

After Mass that morning, Father Pierre met with John Caldwell and Mrs. Julia Dufresne, born Lattier, to join them "in holy and lawful wedlock," with three of their friends serving as witnesses.[58] This eleventh wedding of the year took place in his office, as only Julia was Catholic and she had been married before. With proper dispensation, the brief but joyous ceremony concluded. This was the rhythm of the life of the Church and was perhaps one of the final truly joyful moments of ministry that Father Pierre would have in his remaining earthly life.

It was Providence that kept Father Pierre in Shreveport, as he had already been identified as an excellent candidate for the episcopate. Writing of Father Pierre, Bishop Martin had noted that his "excellent reputation had reached past the limits of [the] humble diocese" of Natchitoches. His mission work and steadfast faith attracted the attention of the hierarchy. In fact, many in the Church were seeking Father Pierre's removal from this minor diocese on the periphery to some more influential corner of the Catholic universe.[59] Bishop Martin's repeated insistence that Father Pierre remain in Shreveport was fortuitous.

On that very evening, September 1, the second-floor office of Civil War veteran and physician Dr. Arie Snell was the site of an important gathering with an urgent purpose. Among those present were physicians, a few of the city's ministers and other prominent citizens. What ensued may have well been a lively debate between the realists who recognized yellow fever and the reluctant who refused its recognition. However, at the evening's conclusion, together they formally (if begrudgingly) proclaimed the active presence of yellow fever in Shreveport.[60] There would be resistance and even public outcry, especially among the merchant class, as everyone in the room knew. Therefore, Shreveport awakened the following day to the mitigated and somewhat softer news of the presence of yellow fever in the city's population but denials that it existed on epidemic scale.

However, out of newspaper headlines and the public eye, the corpses filling the mortuary on a now daily basis spoke a very different truth. There had been, by that twentieth day of the outbreak, already twenty-nine recorded deaths.[61] Even so, the editors of the *Daily Shreveport Times*, whose pledged mission was to steadfastly serve as the "commercial and political paper devoted to the development of the material resources of Northwest Louisiana, Eastern Texas, and Southwest Arkansas," did not acknowledge the situation.[62] The fact that the denial of a yellow fever epidemic was public and circulated meant that some people did not take the precautions they might have otherwise.

Meanwhile, perhaps driven by instinct or intuition or memories of the past, many people began leaving Shreveport, numbering into the hundreds. The day after the acknowledgement of yellow fever's presence in the city, the six-thirty morning train to Texas was fuller than usual. The droves of people rushing the two o'clock afternoon train resembled nothing less than a stampede. This outbound traffic continued unabated for several days: each departing train overflowed as hundreds more anxious residents lined the tracks, awaiting passage. Those who had access simply hitched up wagons or rode on horseback, away from the city and the pestilence. Some packed their steamer trunks and took to the riverboats, which were still running. In a matter of days, Shreveport certainly would have appeared "depopulated," with nearly one-third of its population having fled.[63]

An example of this is found in Leopold Baer, who owned a general mercantile establishment on Texas Street and was among the first to leave in what he believed to be an escape from the illness in early September. Yet,

An illustration that shows how yellow fever outbreaks in the nineteenth century caused people to flee infected areas. *Getty Images.*

unknowingly, he was infected with the virus when he arrived in Marshall, Texas, less than forty miles to the west, where he suffered and then died on September 8.[64] Many others who left were similarly unaware they were infected. Because the mosquito is the required vector for the transmission of the virus in previously unaffected populations, those who fled the city who were already carrying yellow fever may have been the cause of its spread to other locations.

Notable in the narrative, of course, are those who might have had the means to leave but instead chose to stay.

Also present on the evening of September 1 was the physician and rector of Saint Mark's Episcopal Church Reverend Dr. William Tucker Dickinson Dalzell. Having seen yellow fever epidemics in the past, Dalzell skirted the notion of a minor fever problem and instead posted in the September 2 newspaper a request for "the men of Shreveport…to meet in the hall of the Board of Trade…to organize an association for the care and relief of the sick and needy."[65] The meeting was to be held that very morning, such was the urgency of the situation.

At ten o'clock the next morning, September 2, a few citizens came together at the Board of Trade for the public meeting. They gathered "around the green baize covered table, over which trade and railroads and stocks were [once] discussed.[66] The meeting was in the same room where festivities surrounding the opening of the Texas & Pacific Railroad were planned.[67] On this day, a very different kind of community focus prevailed. The grim topic now was the need to organize a charitable response for the ill. Among those around the table was Father Jean Pierre.

Absent from that first meeting was Father Isidore Quémerais, who was one week from his twenty-sixth birthday and recovering from an episode of ill health at the O'Neill home in Bellevue in rural Bossier Parish. However ill he might have been at the time, there can be no question that Father Quémerais immediately responded to Father Pierre's call to return to Shreveport, even as "consumption was consuming him" and he "was not thought to live long."[68] This reliable testimony came from the direct successor of Father Pierre at Holy Trinity Church, Father Joseph Gentille, who made special note of Father Quémerais's condition in his personal diary account of the events and of Quémerais's obedience to the call to serve when it came. He returned to Shreveport to assist Father Pierre out of his own remarkable sense of duty.

Baptized with the name Isidore, the patron saint of farmers, Father Quémerais hailed from the rural village of Pleine-Fougères in the Archdiocese of Rennes. His sharp mind, piety and devotion compensated for whatever he may have lacked in physical stamina. Contributing to his missionary calling was his rather quick mastery of the English language. Father Quémerais, with his rare selfless charisma—he was described as a Franco-Southern gentleman—proved invaluable to Father Pierre in these final days.[69] Their work together, to the point of exhaustion, inevitably links their deaths in the closest of proximities. In fact, it is challenging to separately recount the final days and hours of one's life without mirroring those of the other.

At this September 2 meeting at the Board of Trade, the primary question was how to best care for the "sick-poor": working poor families, freedmen and immigrants. This concern would have been paramount in the mind of Father Jean Pierre, and although the public record is silent, one can imagine that he was a major voice for those who were voiceless in the city's crisis. The community knew of his compassion for the poor, and as one who lived the Gospel call to serve Christ in others, Father Pierre would not have been silent about their special plight. There was no shortage of street urchins, ragmen and tramps with no means of escaping the city, all facing an equalizing fate at the hand of yellow fever.[70]

Although Shreveport had an early concept of a charity hospital for such cases, at this point it remained an idea and not yet the institution that would eventually become a reality for the area. The U.S. Marine Hospital was also not suitable, especially with no guaranteed support from the federal government given the uncertain future of the epidemic. Instead, residents organized a private association, completely reliant on donations, and utilized all the political, social, religious and commercial connections its leaders could muster to respond to the most urgent needs.

From this was born the local chapter of the Howard Association, named for the British social justice pioneer John Howard (1726–1790). Many Howard Association chapters had already formed in the United States in the mid-nineteenth century in response to yellow fever cases elsewhere. They fundraised, organized caregivers and coordinated relief efforts across the South.[71] The Shreveport chapter began with nineteen founding members, including Father Jean Pierre. Within the first of its resolutions was found the following plea: "Anyone who is familiar with the treatment of yellow fever desiring to offer their services as nurses will please give their names."[72]

Although medical relief was perhaps the immediate priority for most of the responders, Father Pierre and Father Quémerais realized there was a greater and more compelling spiritual need for those stricken with yellow fever. They sought also to sanctify plague-ridden Shreveport by continuing the sacraments for Roman Catholics. They offered Mass daily but also prayed with the afflicted, regardless of creed, class or race. They anointed sick Catholics and were simply present for and prayed with all others, many in their final moments of life.

Certainly, the priests witnessed no shortage of burials, and when there was a shortage of workers, the priests no doubt even assisted with the manual task of digging as well. However, in these early weeks of the epidemic, no one foresaw the digging of a trench on the southwest corner of the City Cemetery (today known as Oakland Cemetery) as a single mass grave. At no other time in Shreveport history was the need for compassionate Christian care so crucial as when death loomed so near to so many.

By mid-September, the daily death toll, magnified by the loss of city workers and the collapse of many city services' administrative infrastructure, demanded an efficient and sanitary means of disposing of the dead. In scenes reminiscent of medieval plague-stricken towns, the dead were delivered to the cemetery without ceremony, ritual or accompanying commemorations and placed in a mass grave alongside what would ultimately prove to be nearly eight hundred victims. While it cannot be known from the record whether or not Father Pierre or Father Quémerais attended to the burial of any of these remains in the early days of the trench being opened, they certainly knew of the grim circumstances that surrounded it. As priests of the Church, they prayed daily for the dead.

Meanwhile, in early September, steamers continued to come and go from Shreveport, indifferent to the growing concern ashore or the morbid developments in the city cemetery. In an interesting juxtaposition, the large commercial steamer *Texas* left for New Orleans the same day the Shreveport Howard Association formed as a relief response to a growing health crisis. Throughout the first week of September, business seemingly continued as usual, without regard to the declaration of the presence of yellow fever.[73]

In fact, the *Daily Shreveport Times* continued to report a measure of skepticism about the existence of an epidemic in the face of mounting evidence to the contrary: "From what we learn there is no doubt but the reports of the prevailing sickness in this city are greatly exaggerated abroad."[74] Within its pages, such denials were typeset just inches from reports that the paper's own senior editor, the foreman of the office and three printers were all down with yellow fever, while another staffer was absent because his entire family was stricken.[75]

Meanwhile, the focus of Father Jean Pierre was on the duty that lay before him and his young assistant. His daily routine would have involved praying the Daily Office, celebrating Mass and tending as much as possible to the routine functions of parish life, all the while working in what had been designated Fever Ward 1. (Father Quémerais served in Fever Ward 2.) Father Pierre may have been oblivious to the polarizing outlook of the general public surrounding him. Within the same September 3 edition of the *Daily Shreveport Times*, there were reports of a local druggist posting patients' temperatures daily to monitor the spread of disease, city merchants advertised products dedicated to "convalescing" and the Howard Association published its first mortuary report of yellow fever victims. Three recorded deaths in the city on September 3 were attributed to the disease. The city's Board of Administrators appropriated $500 to purchase medicine and ice and to hire nurses. Relentless in denial, on this day, the newspaper reported, "The fury of the disease seems have expended itself on its victims and to be now dying out. There has been much greater scare than there was cause for....Our advice is to keep cool mentally and physically."[76]

Many theorized the illness was related to poorly serviced outhouses and open pits of sewage.[77] Proponents of this theory were approaching the true cause but did not know exactly how these conditions were related to it. With correlation not equalling causation, uncertainty only continued. No one fathomed the critical link between the life cycle of the mosquito and the conditions in which the insects thrived—or that they could transmit a disease. That connection was not made for three more decades.

In the meantime, the city dealt with the misery of reality in the limited way it could be understood. Leading the efforts in Fever Ward 1 was Father Pierre, passing from one need to the next and one person to the next. He did not count the passing hours of his own life or express concern for his own health. Witnesses reported that he worked until he simply could not stand any longer without rest.

The contrast between the life of the Church and the life of the world may have never appeared more clearly defined than during these twelve weeks of epidemic in the city's history. The required practical civic duties contrasted with the eternal ministrations that may have gone largely unseen and therefore unreported in the public record. This does not make them less significant, only less visible to history—but worthy of consideration here.

As city officials ordered men to spread lime throughout gutters and standing water, the life of the Church spread the invisible gift of hope and light. Those same men of the city placed tar barrels in the streets and burned them to release dense clouds of black smoke, a practice thought to rid the

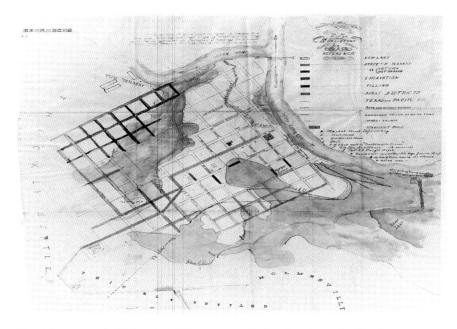

Hand-drawn map by University of Kentucky medical student Augustine Booth, who came to study the yellow fever epidemic of Shreveport shortly after its conclusion. He did not understand how the disease was transmitted but noted interesting features of the epidemic area, including pools of stagnant water. *Noel Archives and Special Collections, Louisiana State University at Shreveport.*

atmosphere of poisonous vapors or "miasma."[78] The fumes indeed helped, somewhat, but by unintentionally repelling mosquitos. Meanwhile, at Holy Trinity, there was comforting contrast in the fragrant smoke of incense, along with prayers Father Pierre and Father Quémerais offered for those buried without a Requiem Mass. Both priests offered the Mass of the Dead and prayed the *De profundis* from the altars in the church where fewer and fewer people were present.

The life in both spheres, temporal and spiritual, manifested in their respective responses amid the shared common reality of physical death.

Sometimes, the imagery of the city must have conjured notions of a visible hell. With the thermometer reaching 87 degrees Fahrenheit on Wednesday, September 3, the plumes of tar turned the city into a reeking furnace. However, Father Pierre, with eight other men, went to work as conditions demanded. The group ranged in age from store clerk Otto Schnurr, seventeen, to J.W. Booth, fifty-three, a painter from England. Two were in the medical field: Dr. W.S. Donaldson, age unknown, and R. Hyams, thirty-

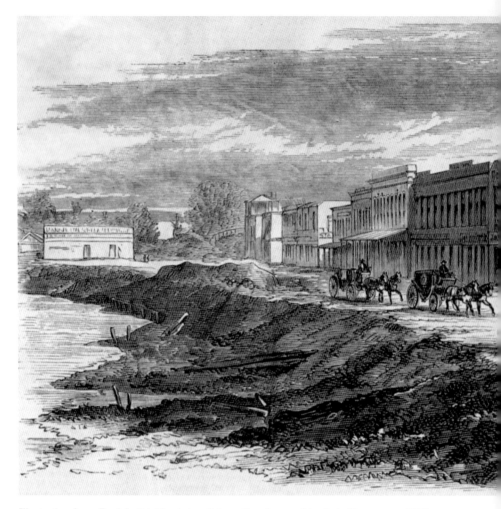

Illustration from *Frank Leslie's Newspaper* of the yellow fever epidemic in Shreveport, 1873. *Authors' collection.*

six, a druggist from South Carolina. L.R. Simmons, thirty years old, a future newspaper editor, served as Howard Association president. Others were R.H. Lindsay, thirty-nine, a cotton factor and immigrant from Scotland; Tom Bylan, forty, ship's carpenter from Ohio; and J.J. Horan, thirty-seven, saddlemaker from Ireland.[79]

Father Pierre and the other volunteers covered twenty-eight blocks, between Common Street and the river, bounded on the other two ends by the north side of Texas Street and Caddo Street. They made no distinction between patients based on class or economic status. Yellow fever spread so

rapidly, and the demand for aid was so pervasive, "there were none so proud that they did not claim assistance; there were none so poor and outcast that its succor did not reach them."[80]

In their first week, the workers in the fever wards nursed, fed and provided basic comfort. When the fever was triumphant, they often shifted to the macabre task of digging graves. The poorest were brought to a temporary hospital established at the opulent opera house, Talley's, on Milam Street in Fever Ward 2.[81] Ironically, a locale noted for its socially elite clientele became a common hospital for all. Like the open trench at the City Cemetery, the opera house became subject to the great social equalizer that was yellow fever.

From the river, approaching traffic would encounter a riverfront cityscape reminiscent of hell. Yet commercial life showed no signs of yielding to the fatal reality ashore. That evening, the steamer *Royal George* arrived with cotton bales from Jefferson, Texas. Two other steamers left Shreveport for New Orleans. While other Gulf of Mexico ports imposed a quarantine against the Crescent City, New Orleans was still allowing traffic from just about anywhere. Shreveport was destined to have contact with the outside world—including its revered river traffic—for but a precious while longer.[82]

While Father Pierre and Father Quémerais labored among the sick, suffering and dying, all the while maintaining their normal duties as best they could, the contrast of unimpeded commercial life must have seemed remote. Their level of physical exhaustion began to mount in the face of the sheer human need before them, so they were likely unaware of many of the news reports surrounding the crisis. In these days, the noose of the quarantine began to tighten as cases spread beyond Shreveport. With panic now spreading throughout east Texas, on Friday morning, September 5, the mayor of Jefferson declared, "This dire disease is raging in Shreveport and would play havoc with us in every way."[83] Shreveport editors responded with several inches of a lead column lambasting the "vicious...rattle brained" editors of Jefferson's paper. The two cities were partners in times of economic prosperity, and their mutual interests were directly at stake.[84]

The ongoing denial of the Shreveport paper, which attributed deaths to "excessive drinking," heart disease and even "swamp fever," rather than yellow fever, contrasted the obvious reality. Meanwhile, single-minded in their compassionate ministry, Father Pierre and Father Quémerais worked night and day. Maybe, one day, they even paused to enjoy a brief glimpse of hope, as there had been fewer than ten interments of victims in the past two days.[85] Father Pierre, in the midst of his selfless service, rose to pastoral leadership for the entire city when he asked that this request be published in the *Daily Shreveport Times*:

> *The undersigned appeals to all those who believe in the efficacy of prayer, and beseeches them to implore God to have pity on us, and if it is His holy will to deliver us from sickness.*
>
> *Respectfully,*
> *Father J. Pierre*

Prayer.

At the request of that worthy and excellent minister, Father Pierre, we insert the following:

The undersigned appeals to all those who believe in the efficacy of prayer, and beseeches them to implore God to have pity on us, and if it is His holy will to deliver us from sickness.

Respectfully,   J. PIERRE.

Father Pierre asked that the *Daily Shreveport Times* print this prayer for the community at the beginning of the epidemic in early September 1873. *Authors' collection.*

Undoubtedly, Father Pierre remembered 1858, after the construction of Holy Trinity Church and during his month-long tenure in Bayou Pierre, when he fell ill with a debilitating unnamed fever. During that illness, he penned a quick and desperate note to Bishop Martin: "I have been sick here for six days, nailed to the bed, still burning with intense fever....If this does not leave me, I ardently desire you send a priest from Natchitoches to give me the last Sacraments."[86] Indeed, although historical observers have made much of Father Quémerais's previous illness and precarious state of health, similar conclusions about Father Pierre's health might be drawn from a reading of his own letters. If he had previously suffered from yellow fever, it might have conferred some immunity. However, such immunity, even if it existed, would have been compromised by the extreme physical demands of working as he did in the fever ward.

Meanwhile, as six more were buried in the City Cemetery, including a traveling circus ringmaster, Dallas and Longview, Texas, established official quarantines.[87] A Texas newspaper correspondent wrote: "There is one awful characteristic about the sickness, and that is, that no one has recovered. Some are what they say doing well. One day you hear of a case doing well.... The next day a corpse is awaiting the hearse."[88] The relapsing course that the newspaper correspondent described was to be exactly the course of the illness for Father Quémerais.

The two priests were likely oblivious to the media attention focused on the crisis in Shreveport. In fact, the entire nation was consumed with events in Shreveport. By mid-September, other city newspapers had begun following the story. By mid-October, even the *New York Times* was reporting that "hundreds have fallen victim to the terrible scourge" and "the fever there [in Shreveport] is of such a malignant type…all who are seized with it drop off like sheep dying with the rot."[89]

Yellow Fever "monster" illustration that expresses the public response to the illness at its epidemic levels. *Library of Congress Prints and Photographs Collection.*

By this time, only outdoor Masses could be celebrated, since public health officials decreed no groups could gather indoors under any circumstances. Father Pierre and Father Quémerais wore the liturgical green and prayed the Mass of the Fourteenth Sunday after Pentecost. The faithful beseeched God's mercy, as their pastor had asked, and sought the protection of the Fourteen Holy Helpers. On this day, Matthew 6:24–33 presented a common theme:

> *Do not worry about your life, what you will eat or drink, or about your body….Can any of you by worrying add a single moment to your life-span?…Seek first the kingdom of God.*

On the ninth of September, Father Isidore Quémerais, with no time to celebrate his twenty-sixth birthday as he had each ninth day of September, prayed the Office and then a private Mass at the side altar of Holy Trinity. People no longer called on the priests, even for important matters. This reality is documented in the sacramental registers of Holy Trinity, for neither Father Pierre nor Father Quémerais made any new entries in September, as there were no baptisms, weddings or funeral Masses.[90] Meanwhile, the *Daily Shreveport Times* relented and confirmed a yellow fever outbreak. The epidemic was almost a month old, and finally, public denials ceased.[91]

During the last week of their lives, both Father Pierre and Father Quémerais went to the bedsides of the wealthy and the poor, anointed the Catholics and whispered comfort to all. The now twenty-six-year-old Father Quémerais spent himself into exhaustion first and sacrificed his own precarious health, having known this was likely from the time he answered Father Pierre's call to return to Shreveport. As his exhaustion overtook him, there were many other new fever cases that day and twelve more burials.[92]

Father Pierre sent an urgent dispatch to Marshall, Texas:[93]

> *Send us all the Sisters of Charity you can spare to our city, as soon as possible. All arrangements will be made to take care of them.*
> *Father J. Pierre*

The sisters based in Marshall, Texas, were ready. Nearer, of course, were the Daughters of the Cross at the convent of Saint Vincent's in Fairfield. With the start of classes postponed, Father Pierre knew the Daughters of the Cross stood ready to assist. However, yellow fever infected the Fairfield convent several days before Father Pierre's dispatch even reached them,

St. Mary's Convent and School, Daughters of the Cross, located very near Holy Trinity Church in downtown Shreveport. This photo dates to 1870. This was the site of the death of Father Pierre on September 16, 1873. *Noel Archives and Special Collections, Louisiana State University at Shreveport.*

affecting those who had not yet had an opportunity to help with nursing. At this point, many of the sisters were too ill to help.[94] In Marshall, the Sisters of Charity answered Father Pierre's call, boarding the Texas & Pacific Railroad. The railroad ignored the quarantine and let the sisters pass to render aid. With the number of volunteers greatly diminished, Shreveport desperately needed the help.

The New Orleans Howard Association, desperate for information, had requested an update from Shreveport on September 10 to determine how best to help with the growing crisis. They received the anticipated response that the city needed nurses and physicians, although there was little hope of paying them. The New Orleans Howards promised to send three physicians and eight nurses the following morning, pledging that the people of New

Orleans would cover their expenses.[95] Father Pierre, although feeling an understandable fatigue, was relieved to hear a second wave of assistance was coming.[96] He did not yet know that his own fatigue foreboded the beginning of his own infection with yellow fever or, at a minimum, predisposed his body to more easily contract it.

Working with Father Pierre but with Father Quémerais more directly was yet another heroic figure of this time in Shreveport. On the river, a parallel sense of duty also gripped Lieutenant Eugene Woodruff. He joined the fight against the disease in Fever Ward 2, leaving his brother George and his crew behind on the snag boat *Aid*. Woodruff volunteered with the Howards and began organizing the hospital in Talley's Opera House. His efforts overlapped with those of Father Quémerais, and undoubtedly, the two men knew each other.[97] In a letter Woodruff wrote to his mother in Iowa on September 9, the date Father Quémerais would have otherwise celebrated his birthday, he had shrugged off the danger facing them all, reassuring her:

> *We are all in excellent health.…I do not consider myself in any danger for two reasons. First my life insurance policy is made to cover the risk by a permit received in June from the home company. Second, my system is in good condition to resist attacks, and I am not in the least afraid.…For myself you need not worry.*[98]

So resolute was Woodruff to remain in Shreveport that he refused the army's order to leave until the epidemic passed. He died on September 30 of yellow fever while caring for other victims.

Meanwhile, two miles south of Shreveport and far inland from the infested riverfront, Father Jean Marie Biler, chaplain to the Daughters of the Cross, was also on the front lines fighting despair. A messenger raced to the Fairfield convent on Tuesday, September 9, with a new appeal from Father Pierre to Mother Mary Hyacinth for as many sisters as she could spare to assist.[99] The messenger also carried a second letter from Father Pierre that was addressed specifically to Father Biler, begging for his help. Father Pierre knew that both he and Father Quémerais faced complete exhaustion and, at this point, may have indeed already surmised that they had each contracted the fever.[100] Immediately after Mass, Father Biler headed to the fever wards to join Father Quémerais and Father Pierre.[101] With no thought of his own life or welfare, yet another priest turned his face toward death-ridden Shreveport.

Reinforcing their efforts were Sister Mary of the Cross and Sister Mary Angela, who had been at Saint Mary's since early September. At Father Pierre's request, Mother Superior sent others: Sister Mary Seraphina, Sister Mary Vincent and Sister Mary Martha.[102] Sister Mary Martha soon ministered with Father Pierre. Also a native of France, Sister Mary Martha was born in 1828 and baptized Marie Françoise Déné. She was an original member of the Daughters of the Cross who came to the United States in 1855.[103]

Shreveport was increasingly isolated from the outside world; the *Times* itself reported its inability to keep citizens apprised. "Owing to the want of compositors, we are unable to issue more than a half sheet for the present. We will do better as soon as the epidemic will permit. As it is, we are doing well to get even that out." The newspaper's staff dwindled due to the effects wrought by the illness. Ironically, this punctuated the very epidemic that the editors adamantly denied just a week before.[104]

By the second full week of September, interments were so frequent that the dead received no ceremony. Volunteers had buried approximately 120 residents since September began, a figure that did not include deceased refugees.[105] With exhaustion setting in among the dwindling volunteers, the dying required more care than the living could offer. The three priests took turns commending souls to the Lord and then blessing and sprinkling with holy water the bodies in the mass grave at the City Cemetery. The *New York Times* later reprinted this account from a Shreveport resident:

> *We no longer* [have] *funerals; the hearses, followed by one or two carriages,* [dash] *through the streets like sections of artillery in a battle seeking a position; enough men* [are] *drummed up, often with difficulty, to lift the coffin into the hearse and the body* [is] *borne away to the cemetery as swiftly as decency…permit*[s].[106]

On September 12, the sky drew up in a curtain of gray cloud cover that unleashed a "fine thunder shower accompanied by a copious rain."[107] From his home in Fever Ward 4 off Fairfield Avenue, between Saint Vincent's and the commercialized town, Caddo Parish Judge Henry Gerard Hall, with little work to be done as no trials were scheduled, used his free time to write in his diary, an account that helps frame the final days of Father Pierre and Father Quémerais in some context. Noting the rainfall, Judge Hall expressed the ironic hope that it would stop the spread of sickness. Little did anyone know that quite the opposite was certain.

The "great blessing" of a "bountiful rain" that filled the judge's cistern and prompted the hopeful notice of the *Daily Shreveport Times* brought other unwanted effects. The rains produced stagnant pools; widened the

Nineteenth-century illustration characterizing yellow fever by its often-quoted nickname, Yellow Jack. *Library of Congress Prints and Photographs Collection.*

muddy lowlands, which were soon teeming with mosquito larvae; and also extinguished the burning tar barrels. The life cycle of the mosquito *Aedes aegypti* meant that the many eggs laid following the rain would form adult mosquitoes within a few days. The bountiful rain produced new breeding grounds for the mosquitos.

Henceforth, commercial contact further slowed, and telegraph communications became even less frequent, but understanding the mosquito vector allows some insight into why this occurred. The public record continued to provide a mostly accurate death count and the names of the deceased, but such news only heightened the anxiety and suffering of Shreveport. Those who were not physically ill were certainly emotionally and spiritually afflicted—if not by direct personal loss, then by fear.

"Good Father Biler," as Mother Superior called him, returned to the convent on Saturday evening, September 13, for a retreat with the Sisters, who prepared to solemnly renew their Holy Vows.[108] Their joy at seeing him quickly turned to concern, for he "brought the sad news that Father Pierre was unwell and Father Quémerais completely exhausted from fatigue."[109] The convent's chaplain ate a light supper and then returned to town, promising he would be back at the convent the next morning for Sunday Mass.

THE SCOURGE OF YELLOW FEVER.

SCENES IN SHREVEPORT, LA.

THE intelligence received from Shreveport, La., during the past week, was extremely distressing. Few cities in the South enjoyed fairer prospects of an immediate commercial activity. As recently as August 13th, a grand jubilee was held within the limits of this now fever-stricken city, as a celebration of the completion of the Texas and Pacific Railroad to Dallas, Texas. It was then thought that the two cities, Dallas, Texas, and Shreveport, La., were about assuming very important relations with the large commercial marts of the country. The Fall crops promised to be unusually large, and it was considered that the greater portion raised in those States would seek an outlet at these cities. One month later, and yellow fever, that fearful scourge, settled upon the place. But two reasons have so far been assigned for its appearance. One authority charges it upon the members of a Mexican circus troupe, another thinks its prevalence is owing to the unusually heavy float of timber and rafts down the Red River.

The stricken city is situated on the west bank of Red River, in the northern part of Louisiana, about three hundred miles by land northwest of Baton Rouge, and about thirty miles below the "Great Raft," which is the limit of navigation for large steamboats. It is a thriving town, and previous to its present isolation had daily communication by water and railway with New Orleans and all parts of the country. A large business has been carried on at Shreveport, as it is advantageously situated for the shipment of cattle from Texas, and of cotton from Louisiana. The population is about 4,6.. of which 2,439 are white and 2,168 colored.

A correspondent, writing on the 6th of Septe.. ber, says:

"The town is nearly depopulated by a stampe.. and sickness. There has been, as near as I c.. ascertain up to date, about sixty people dead.. a great number sick. There is one awful cha.. teristic about the sickness, and that is, that no.. has as yet recovered. Some are what they..

THE HOUSEHOLD HOSF..

Illustration from *Frank Leslie's Newspaper* of the yellow fever epidemic in Shreveport, 1873. *Authors' collection.*

80

ng well, while others die. One day you hear of ase doing as well as could be expected, the next a corpse is awaiting the hearse. On the point malignant fatality it surpasses any yellow fever r known here. It appears as if once the fell aster ever gets its pestilential fangs on its victim, it

Association, and they are doing a great deal of good. Of the fever, I may say that it is different from any yellow fever ever seen here."

On the 7th it was rumored that the Central, International, Great Northern, and Texas and Pacific Railroad Companies were blockaded by the disease. A panic broke out in Galveston and Houston, Texas, and the northbound trains were crowded with citizens fleeing from the scourge. The interior parts of Shreveport were also quarantined on the 7th

The disease spread rapidly, and many deaths occurred. On the 11th the Board of Health of Memphis, Tenn., reported nine deaths from yellow fever at that city, and it was feared the epidemic would gain a more extensive scope. The local Howard Association, the Odd Fellows and Masons, organized relief committees, to be prepared for an emergency.

The number of interments from September 1st to 16th, in Shreveport, was 226, while the number of the sick was estimated at from 500 to 800. On the 14th there was a sudden change in the weather, which increased the alarm. Four days later, large quantities of tar were burned in the streets, and the gas was allowed to escape from the street-lamps. The scourge spread from the low grounds, near the Wolf River, towards the suburbs. On the 16th it was reported at Fulton, the terminus of the Cairo and Fulton Railroad, and at several towns in Northern Louisiana. At Vernon, La., ten circus men died of the fever on the 16th. On the 17th it broke out at Key West, on the United States steamer *Pawnee*, and Lieutenant-Commander Mitchell died from its effects.

LAST OF THE FAMILY.

r lets go its fatal grip until the poor wretch is stiff, dead. A few cases at first dropped dead in the ts before reaching a house. These cases, however, have been rare. We have organized a Howard

The authorities at once set about relieving the distress of the sufferers, but in a short time

Indeed, on Sunday, September 14, Father Quémerais could not rise from bed, so great was his fatigue. He was a priest without a Mass, and it was a Sunday without a homily. Father Pierre, also fatigued, was determined to celebrate the Sunday Mass for his people, who had begun to express a benign acceptance of the constant presence of death.

The one constant thing besides death was the incessant rainfall. That week, the predictable afternoon showers cleaned the atmosphere and fell upon those yet living. The cycle of death continued, aided by the cycle of rain and the life cycle of the mosquitos.

Father Pierre was undoubtedly anxious about his assistant and therefore found it impossible to rest on Sunday, although already clearly ill himself. Father Biler's reports to the sisters at Fairfield indicate that Father Pierre had worked far beyond his human capacity and this had exacted its toll. His offering had been willing, for in the previous week, he and Sister Mary Martha walked within the quarantine bravely and tirelessly. The two stepped onto porches, knocked on doors and, when they opened, entered to go to the bedsides of those in need.

In a time when the mode of transmission was unknown, they did not fear contracting the illness, even though it was assumed to be person-to-person transmittable. They abandoned all concern for their own safety as they wiped the foreheads and held the hands of the dying, praying with them. They knew they were in the presence of the disease and yet feared not for themselves. Fear fled in the light of the higher call, which was to serve those in need before them. They were heeding Christ's command, in Matthew 25, to visit the sick, believing that as often as they cared for them, they were caring for Jesus Himself.

During one such visit, a frantic father thrust his baby girl into Sister Mary Martha's arms. As Father Pierre prayed at the bedside of the sick mother, the newborn died in Sister's arms.[110] This emotional visit made such an impression that they took time from the day's work to write about it before proceeding to the next house. The pace of the work exacted a toll on them both.

Great uncertainty gripped the city, including those who worked among the sick and dying. It was an easier task to simply count the bodies than to ensure accuracy in the death record. The daily mortuary report furnished by the Howard Association became the primary measuring stick of the epidemic's strength. Were there more dead than yesterday? Yes? The fever is on the rise. No? The fever is drawing to a close. The result was a constant cycle of hope and despair, dependent on mere accounting. Meanwhile, both the wealthy and the poor were drawn to final rest, and their ends came in a ceaseless and ceremony-free procession. For the city's prominent, "death brought down the scepter to the level of the spade."[111]

Father Biler returned as promised in the early morning on September 14 to offer Sunday Mass for the sisters, to lead them in the Ceremony of the Renewal of their Holy Vows and to expose, as was their custom, the Blessed Sacrament in the monstrance for adoration throughout the day.[112] Meanwhile, Father Quémerais, who had selflessly labored to the point of exhaustion, agreed to cease only when a physician ordered him to bed rest; his diagnosis was subsequently confirmed as yellow fever.[113] Although Father Quémerais had been in Shreveport only a short while, the small Catholic community seemingly clung to every update on his condition. The condition of the young priest, which was indeed worrying to all, was symbolic, even, of the fate of the young town on the verge of collapse. Available medicines may have helped relieve his pain, but Father Quémerais offered his suffering, as he told many others to do, for the good of the souls in purgatory. Meanwhile, Father Pierre's condition worsened as well, and the two priests approached eternity within a day of each other, in the shared resolve that their offering of life was the greatest love.

With yellow fever, the actual fever phase normally lasts about seventy-two hours. Some infected were overwhelmed by the violent intensity of the attack, and those, mercifully, died quickly—perhaps by the end of the second day. The young Father Quémerais lingered far longer. Following a sudden end of fever, his dying body transitioned into the "calm stage," his convulsions ceasing and pulse dropping below the average rate.[114] Caregivers could only give him ice to chew on and hope that his would be one of the cases to recover.

The local paper punctuated the situation in dramatic terms: "Shreveport is one great hospital, one great charnel house, and the *Times*, merely a death record."[115] "One great charnel house": Shreveporters knew this archaic term for a place where human remains are stored, in the absence of either propriety or ceremony, sometimes connoting disrespect or lack of concern for the dead.

However, the Shreveport charnel house reflected not disrespect for the dead but rather the inability to properly care for them due to the sheer magnitude of the epidemic. Shreveport was reduced to such careless disposal of remains that every negative image of history was conjured up. The charnel house priests of Shreveport worked *in persona Christi*, in the context of widespread human suffering, with no thought for themselves.

As his assistant's condition briefly stabilized, Father Pierre's worsened. As recorded by observers and later noted in an account by Bishop Martin, Father Pierre stubbornly "refused to go to bed when so many were pleading the consolation of the Church in their last hours."[116] Father Pierre would not allow the city to be without the sacraments, repeating a theme of his ministry he had first expressed many years before. Father Pierre's concern was always that the people would never want for the grace of the sacraments.

The Feast of the Exaltation of the Holy Cross calls the faithful to contemplate the mysteries of the Cross, the meaning of suffering and its ultimate triumph. The fifteenth Sunday after Pentecost providentially fell on the calendar date of September 14. All the Church recognized that on this day every year since the seventh century, the glory of the Cross had been remembered, as the first words of the Mass directed them to do through the *Introit*. The *Collect* was prayed: "May we who have known mystery [of the cross] on earth, also be worthy to enjoy in heaven the happiness which it has purchased for us."[117] As he read aloud the epistle, Father Pierre prayed that they all would be as obedient to death by yellow fever as Jesus was obedient unto death on a cross, if it was to be the will of God.[118] Each prayer fortified those present: "O Lord our God, we are preparing to receive the Body and Blood of our Lord Jesus Christ.…Grant that we may also enjoy for all eternity the salvation it has purchased for us." As the Masses concluded in both Shreveport and Fairfield, they prayed: "Be close to us, O Lord our God."

Although by now severely ill with yellow fever and certainly fighting against the fatigue that demanded he relent physically and withdraw to bed rest, Father Pierre nevertheless celebrated the Mass as if it were his first Mass, his only Mass, his last Mass.

In fact, it was indeed to be his last Mass.

Following Mass at the convent that Sunday, Father Biler quickly ate breakfast and hastened back to town, saying he would return in the evening for Benediction.[119] After Mass at Holy Trinity, Father Pierre was determined to ensure that every Catholic who needed the Last Rites received them, fatigued though he was. Father Quémerais's condition remained such that Father Pierre did not anoint him, as he was in the indeterminate calm state and might yet recover. Shortly thereafter, fever seized Father Pierre just as his assistant also took a turn for the worse. The unimaginable happened: both priests were deathly ill at the same time, bedridden at Saint Mary's Convent near Holy Trinity Church.

Detail of stained-glass window at Holy Trinity Church in Shreveport commemorating Father Jean Pierre. *Authors' collection.*

However, word of Father Pierre's diagnosis did not reach Father Biler before he departed to return to Fairfield, so he arrived back among the sisters at seven o'clock, bringing only the certain news that Father Quémerais had a very critical case of yellow fever. He was not aware of Father Pierre's serious condition at the time.[120]

While the public received the news the next day that Father Pierre was "dangerously sick," he was in fact already in a terminal state. The newspaper lauded his heroism and anticipated his death, calling it "deplored" by the people even before he passed on. Meanwhile, Father Biler continued working at a constant, maddening pace, the impossible work of three priests now left to only one.[121] In his turn, Father Biler also devoted every moment to comforting the sick and dying, imitating the dying priests by resting only when he, too, collapsed.

On Monday morning, September 15, Father Quémerais took a final turn and relapsed. His body temperature spiked again, the convulsions returned and he began to vomit blood, the most ominous of signs.[122] His caregivers gave him as much ice as he would take and caressed his hot, dry skin. The headache would remain to the end, ever more agonizing in its intensity as death drew nearer.

Father Biler came to his bedside with holy water and the *Rituale Romanum*, to anoint his fellow Breton and brother priest. Father Biler could not rouse Father Quémerais as he was unconscious:

> Je suis ici. *I am here, your brother, Jean Marie. Isidore, I prepare you to meet your Redeemer. Kiss the holy crucifix.*
>
> Je suis ici, ton frère, Jean Marie. Isidore, je te prépare à rencontrer ton Rédempteur. Embrasse le saint crucifix.

Father Biler sprinkled holy water in the form of a cross on Father Quémerais and then the room and those standing by, saying in Latin:

> Aspérges me, Dómine…. *"Purify me with hyssop, Lord, and I shall be clean of sin. Wash me, and I shall be whiter than snow." —Psalm 51*

He lit a candle and said in the language of the Church: "Our help is in the name of the Lord." Everyone responded without hesitation: "Who made heaven and earth."

Father Biler continued the ritual:

> *Lord Jesus Christ, let your angels of peace take over and put down all wicked strife. May almighty God have mercy on you, forgive you your sins, and lead you to everlasting life. May the almighty and merciful Lord grant you pardon, absolution, and remission of your sins.*

He dipped his thumb in the holy oil and traced the sign of the cross on Father Quémerais's eyelids, asking mercy for any evil done through the power of sight. Likewise, he anointed each ear, for sins committed through the power of hearing. And then his nose and mouth. He then took Father Quémerais's hands and, for the first time, in an act reserved for moribund priests, anointed the back of the hands—not the palms, as he had done for so many of the laity of late—and then his feet. He prayed the litany:

> Kýrie eléison. Christe eléison. Kýrie eléison.
> *Holy Mary, pray for him.*
> *All holy angels and archangels, pray for him.*
> *Holy Abel,*
> *All choirs of the just,*
> *Holy Abraham,*
> *St. John the Baptist,*
> *St. Joseph,*
> *All holy patriarchs and prophets,*
> *St. Peter,*
> *St. Paul,*
> *St. Andrew,*
> *St. John,*
> *All holy apostles and evangelists,*
> *All holy disciples of our Lord,*
> *All holy Innocents,*
> *St. Stephen,*
> *St. Lawrence,*
> *All holy martyrs....*
> *By the authority granted me by the Holy See, I impart to you a plenary indulgence and the remission of all your sins; and I bless you in the name of the Father, and of the Son, and of the Holy Spirit. Amen.*

With the sign of the cross at the ritual's conclusion, Father Biler spoke words of consolation. "Isidore, resist the temptations of the devil, and if death comes, go peacefully in the Lord." Before he departed for Fairfield, Father Biler commended Father Quémerais's soul to God, as death was imminent. He informed the sisters that he had administered the final sacraments to Father Quémerais but did not remain with him at his bedside due to his own crippling fatigue.[123] Only later did they learn that "the good young priest died at 7 o'clock the evening of the 15th."

The other bad news Father Biler announced was that their dear Sister Mary Martha, the one into whose arms was thrust the dying infant just the week before, also had yellow fever. Father Biler reported that he had no appetite, but at Mother's insistence, he tried to take some supper before making funeral arrangements for Father Quémerais.[124] The prayers of that evening must have been fervent ones, that Father Pierre, still clinging to life at Saint Mary's downtown, would recover his life, along with Sister Mary Martha—but against all odds.

Tuesday, September 16, 1873, marked the Memorial of Saints Cornelius (pope) and Cyprian (bishop), both martyrs of the early Church. At the dawn of that day, Father Pierre clung to his earthly life as a martyr to his charity. With little sleep and already ill himself, Father Biler reentered the quarantine to bury Father Quémerais. He had a brief Requiem Mass, but unlike hundreds of yellow fever victims whose final resting place was a mass grave without ceremony, the young priest from Pleine-Fougères received a proper and dignified, albeit hasty, burial in the City Cemetery. Not far from the mass grave, he was placed in a private plot donated by grieving parishioners.[125]

Later that day, when doctors despaired of saving "dear Father Pierre," Father Biler went to his bedside and, for the second day in a row, anointed the back of two hands and prayed the Litany of Saints.[126] As Father Pierre was conscious, Father Biler offered him Holy Communion as *viaticum*, food for the journey. Father Biler stayed with him until the end. When Father Pierre expressed surprise that Father Quémerais did not visit him, it was Dr. Joseph Moore who informed him, "Father Quémerais has preceded you to Heaven; you will soon go to see him."[127]

Father Biler added the commendation prayers meant for a person literally at the moment of death, which he could not pray for Father Quémerais the day prior:

> *Depart, Christian soul, from this world,*
> *in the name of God the Father almighty who created you;*
> *in the name of Jesus Christ, Son of the living God, who suffered for you;*
> *in the name of the Holy Spirit who sanctified you;*
> *in the name of the glorious and blessed Virgin Mary, Mother of God;*
> *in the name of St. Joseph, her illustrious spouse;*
> *in the name of the Angels and Archangels, Thrones and Dominations, Principalities and Powers, Cherubim and Seraphim;*
> *in the name of the patriarchs and prophets, the holy apostles and evangelists, the holy martyrs and confessors, the holy monks and hermits;*
> *in the name of the holy virgins and all the holy men and women of God.*
> *May you rest in peace this day and your abode be in holy Zion;*
> *through Christ our Lord. Amen.*

"The beautiful soul of the zealous pastor of Holy Trinity took its flight to a better world 24 hours after Father Quémerais," as Mother Mary Hyacinth wrote to the novitiate in France just three days later.[128] Father Jean Pierre was then interred beneath Holy Trinity Church, which he had so lovingly built with the work of his hands, heart and mind.

CHAPTER 4

DEVOTION AND PUBLIC MEMORY

The passing of Father Jean Pierre, following just twenty-four hours after the death of his young assistant, assuredly brought an even deeper pall of despair upon an already grieving city. On the same day that his body was lowered into the ground beneath the church he built, the *Daily Shreveport Times* openly declared itself reduced to nothing more than a public death record. Yet on the front page appeared a column dedicated to news about the condition of notable fever victims. Solemnly recorded among the honored dead—and presented with the simple heading "Catholic Priests"— was Father Isidore Armand Quémerais, just twenty-six years old and yet a "very worthy priest." Father Pierre's death was not yet recorded, speaking to the general chaos of the time.[129]

Father Quémerais had died on the final day of the octave of the Nativity of the Blessed Virgin Mary, a day to reflect on her Seven Sorrows, a day known to the secular world as simply Monday, September 15, 1873. "Practicing the charity that immolates [Jesus Christ]," Father Quémerais died a martyr to his charity in the service of the sick and dying, and as Bishop Auguste Martin later observed, "the angels gathered him for heaven."[130]

The memory of Father Jean Pierre became quickly cemented into the narratives of Shreveport history. When Shreveport residents realized his genuine goodness, even though he represented a distinctly minority faith, he received "money in abundance" from those convinced he would use it prudently. Following his death, an inventory of his personal effects revealed he was virtually penniless. He gave away all he earned as offerings to the poor and to enhance the Church.[131] The bishop himself acknowledged him as "one of the most saintly priests" he had known in his many years of ministry.[132] The Shreveport Howard Association immediately passed a poignant resolution, the first of only a few, as a memorial of his tireless service and sacrifice to people in need.[133]

Father Pierre's place in the public memory was solidly anchored by the actions of the *Daily Shreveport Times*, which published an entire column on its front page just days after his death, during a time when observers reported little news. The obituary was the paper's first to set aside the death of one individual from the simple rosters of the dead, given its own place in the annals of the epidemic. It was a true recounting of a life in the service of others, reflecting the public love of this priest:

Father Pierre

The ministrations and sympathies for our people have been so completely monopolized by the suffering of the sick and the destitution of the poor, that there has been but little time to bewail the dead. Yet we believe we may pause in the midst of the solemn scenes that surround us: that we may snatch a moment from the busy carnival of misery to express the deep regret of this community at the death of the Reverend Father Pierre. This pious priest, kindly and most excellent man, was seized of the fever Saturday evening and died Tuesday evening. From the beginning of the epidemic to the moment he was stricken down, he was constantly engaged in visiting the sick and dying. In these holy ministrations he knew no sects and orders of society, but was found at the bedside of Jew and Gentile, rich and poor. Those who trusted in the religion of Christ and walked in its light, and those whose souls were darkened by crime; the lady and the courtesan, the good and the bad, when suffering with the scourge and smitten with death, found Father Pierre beside them, smoothing their pillows with a womanly tenderness, and consoling them with words of hope.

We believe that the voices of this people, regardless of sect or race, will join in one common expression of regret at the loss of the good Priest, and that amongst us it is the universal opinion that the Christian religion has lost a worthy minister, poor humanity a true friend, and Shreveport a valued and useful citizen.

When the sad era, in the midst of which we now are, shall have passed away, and we have more leisure to devote to the merits of the dead, and more time to indulge our sympathies and tears, we trust that some worthier pen than our own, will do the life of Father Pierre, that high justice it so richly merits.[134]

Other newspapers across the United States reported on Father Pierre's illness even before his death, including the *Philadelphia Inquirer*, the *Daily Press Herald of Knoxville*, the *New Orleans Republican*, the *Vicksburg Herald* and the *Galveston Daily News*, no doubt reflecting the emotional nature of the news coming out of Shreveport as community awareness spread that their beloved Father Pierre was gravely ill.

Numerous secondary accounts, including from other news sources, also attest to the high level of general public esteem for Father Pierre. In fact, the city of Shreveport, with its mostly Protestant and Jewish population, named a street in his honor—Pierre Avenue, appearing consistently on maps of the city by 1885.

Writing to Father Joseph Gentille on October 14, 1873, Bishop Martin referred to Father Pierre as "an admirable model of every priestly virtue." In Father Pierre's last will and testament, he left all of his worldly possessions to the use of his bishop and to further the work of Holy Mother Church. Indeed, although he left Holy Trinity in excellent financial condition, Father Pierre had little to his own name at the time of his death. The bishop paid tribute to Father Pierre's well-known generosity in a letter to Father Gentille on October 31, in which he recounted practical affairs that yet extol the priest:

> *Father Pierre left a will assigning everything to the church. You will find a well-built house and the horse of your confrere. The stable alone needs renovating....You can count on being received (in Shreveport) as an angel from God.*[135]

There is perhaps no one who mourned the loss of Father Pierre more than Bishop Auguste Martin. Across twenty years as bishop of a diocese reliant on missionaries, Bishop Martin became quite accustomed to writing to the Society for the Propagation of the Faith in Paris with reports on the life of his diocese. With joy, he often wrote about steady growth—from five clergymen, seven churches, one religious order and one school when he was ordained in November 1853 to twenty-nine clergy, twenty-six churches and chapels, eight religious orders and seventeen schools by 1873.

Bishop Martin's October 1873 report was quite different. This was to be a letter of "the losses and the sorrows." "Inscrutable, truly, are the ways of the Lord. I adore them and I accept them with my whole soul," he wrote to the Society in Paris, mourning "the irreparable losses" to his diocese and his own personal pain caused by the Shreveport yellow fever epidemic. The letter actually serves as a eulogy to all five priests who heroically died in the epidemic, including Father Jean Pierre.

> *Gentlemen:*
>
> *You may have learned from the Paris newspapers that a pestilential fever, with a deadliness heretofore unknown in Louisiana, broke out about the end of August in Shreveport, a commercial city of ten thousand, in the extreme northwest of my diocese. There it caused and continues to cause dreadful ravages, the extent of which we will not know until later. That which the newspapers could not tell you, gentlemen, is of the irreparable losses to my diocese and my pain as bishop, in seeing fall, in the space of three weeks, five of my priests and among them the three most eminent members of my clergy. In a rare assemblage of priestly virtues, of science and of talents, three had joined the Mission in 1854 and had reached maturity while producing an apostolic career filled with work and rich in the fruits of life which will live after them.*

The lengthy narrative continued to consider the personal sacrifice of each "martyr to his charity." Bishop Martin memorialized each priest with a mix of prose that included a practical recounting of their ministries and praise for their virtues and even offered glimpses into their personalities. They had labored together, they were his friends and he wrote of them as such.

> *The first victim chosen by God was Mr. Isidore Quémerais, age 26, from the Diocese of Rennes, vicar in Shreveport. Mr. Father Quémerais was one of the seven young Bretons who followed me to Louisiana on my return from the Vatican Council. The piety, the gentleness, the unselfish dedication of this young priest, his filial affection for his bishop and the ease with which he mastered the difficulties of the English language permitted me to place great hope in him for the future. This was a flower; the angels gathered him for heaven. After two years of his ministry and while practicing the charity that immolates, he died on September 15th.*
>
> *The next day marked the death of one of the most saintly priests that I have known in my long career: Mr. Father Pierre, founder of the missions in Bayou Pierre, Minden and Shreveport, whom you will learn more about from the account of his life and work, published in the* Catholic Propagator, *which I have the honor of sending you. Long since, his excellent reputation had reached past the limits of my humble diocese, and to keep such a treasure, it was necessary, more than once, to defend him*

against the truly justified esteem of several of my venerable colleagues, who saw in him a worthy candidate for the episcopate. The good Lord had given us this treasure; he has taken him away; may his Holy Name be blessed.

On the 26th Mr. Father Biler died. He was chaplain of the novitiate and boarding school of the Daughters of the Cross at Fairfield. This excellent priest, 33 years old, from the Diocese of Saint-Brieuc et Tréguier, had been in our mission only two and a half years. He had given up everything in Brittany, through the entreaties of Rev. Mother Le Conniat, his relative, to dedicate himself to this establishment to which it was impossible for me to provide a priest. At the first news of the illness of his confreres, he went to them, appointed himself their guardian, assisted them in their last moments and blessed their tombs. Left alone at the height of the plague, he called upon the charity of Messrs. Father Gergaud and Father Le Vézouët. The first arrived only a few days later to see him fall in his turn and to provide him with the consolations which he had given to the others at the expense of his own precious life.

Mr. Father Gergaud, from the Diocese of Nantes, ordained a priest for the diocese of Natchitoches in 1854, founder and pastor of the mission of Monroe for eighteen years, Vicar Forane, appointed by the bishop, for all the districts situated between the Mississippi and the Red River valley, was a true "Homo Dei." Endowed with a very energetic nature, an elevated and cultivated spirit, patient and ardent zeal, a tender and generous heart protected by a prudent and reserved manner, Mr. Father Gergaud was a torch spreading light and heat around him. In a place where never before had a priest resided, where I had nothing to offer him but the unfinished skeleton of a chapel and a few diffident Christians and where I doubted that he could live, Mr. Father Gergaud founded and leaves behind him a flourishing mission: church, presbytery, convent, Catholic school for boys, a large cemetery for the exclusive use of the faithful—he created it all, and in a period of eighteen years, his expenses for the honor of the religion exceeded two hundred thousand francs, of which I had allocated him barely ten thousand from the society. It is because his faith, while giving him the courage for any undertaking, also gave him the power to open the hearts and instill some of the generosity of his own soul. Through his outstanding talents, his priestly virtues and his work, Mr. Father Gergaud was a veritable power in Monroe, and because of his incontestable superiority, he was the leader of the diocesan clergy. At the time of the last Provincial Council, to which he accompanied me as a theologian, I nominated him to my venerable colleagues, and he was readily accepted as my successor to the see of Natchitoches. Such a great consolation was to be denied me.

Upon receiving Mr. Father Biler's letter calling him to his aid, Mr. Father Gergaud left without a moment's hesitation. His only directive to his assistant, Mr. Quelard, was: "Write to Monseigneur at once; tell him that I am going to my death, that it is my duty and that I am leaving." He lived only ten days in Shreveport. Welcomed by all as a Godsent angel, he overextended himself during one week to satisfy all the needs; he exerted himself beyond measure. There were more than one thousand sick people; of that number, perhaps fewer than twenty-five were Catholic; but in the presence of death, it was the priest that everyone called for, and God alone knows how many souls owe their salvation to the heroism of the Catholic priest. Meanwhile, Mr. Father Biler was stricken; he died on the 27th, assisted by Mr. Father Gergaud. The following day Mr. Father Gergaud was also mortally stricken, and he died on October 1st, consoled and purified by the ministrations of one of his holiest and best-loved confreres, Mr. Father Le Vézouët, who, like the others, was a victim destined for death.

Mr. Father Le Vézouët, from a very Christian family of wealthy farmers of the Diocese of Saint-Brieuc et Tréguier, was endowed with a wide-ranging intelligence and a keen imagination. He had completed a brilliant course of classical and scientific studies and passed, with distinction, the examinations then required by the university for almost all the liberal arts. Among all the careers open to him, he chose the serious and dedicated life of the priesthood and had completed his theological studies when, in 1854, he asked to follow me. After eighteen months of strengthening himself in his studies and in learning English, which he mastered easily, his talent for drawing young people to himself and his remarkable aptitude for teaching made me decide to entrust to him very particularly the religious instruction and spiritual direction of St. Joseph College, which I was establishing at Natchitoches in 1856 and in which, at the same time, he was teaching several classes. Shortly after, the president having retired, he succeeded him, and with great zeal and success he directed, until 1862, the establishment which, in that disastrous time, was completely devastated and ruined by the successive invasions of two belligerent armies. Hardly had he been relieved of the direction and his teaching at the college when I entrusted him with the evangelization of the poor and degraded Mexicans, spread out between the Red River and the Sabine, whose language he spoke with ease. Although he usually resided in Natchitoches, where his presence had become indispensable to me, he regularly fulfilled this difficult Mission with the dedicated zeal that he brought to everything that he undertook; he did this as an apostle for nine years, instructing the people, validating marriages, building and furnishing churches, and by the Divine Word and the grace of the sacraments, he elevated these unrefined people to the dignity of Christians. Finally, as his crowning achievement in this work, in 1871, he founded a permanent mission in Many, at the very center of this population. There he constructed a church with its presbytery, its cemetery, the lands necessary for the residence of a priest, and he even installed, in the same year, a young confrere, successor of his zeal. Here Mr. Father Le Vézouët was one of the three members of the episcopal council, diocesan director and zealous promoter of the works of the Propagation of the Faith and the Holy Childhood, chaplain of the convent of the Sisters of Mercy and director of a day school which he founded for boys, responsible, moreover, for several small missions at a short distance from Natchitoches, for preaching in English at the Cathedral and for a large number of penitents. But above all, Mr. Father Le Vézouët was the friend, the consoler, the priest of the children, of the afflicted and of the poor. Whatever time these rigid demands left to him, he used for them, he spent with them, going from cabin to cabin, bringing encouragement, consolation and alms to all.

On September 19th, Mr. Father Le Vézouët returned to Natchitoches after an eight-day mission on the left bank of the Red River. After having told him of Mr. Father Biler's request to me that he be sent immediately to Shreveport, I asked him, "What would you like to do, my son?" He replied, "Monseigneur, if you tell me to leave, I leave; if you leave it up to me, I stay." He realized that I was searching his eyes for the real meaning of his response, and he added: "I want to go so much that if you left the decision up to me, I would believe that in going, I was acting according to my own will, and I do not want to do anything but the will of God." "If it is so," I replied to him, "go." He spent one more day putting his affairs in order and visiting several families for the last time. The news of his imminent departure spread quickly, and to those who said, "You are going to your death," he replied, "I believe it, but I know that I am taking the surest and the shortest path to heaven." Because other means of transportation were lacking, Mr. Father Le Vézouët had to undertake the 110-mile journey to Shreveport on horseback. He arrived there to find Mr. Father Gergaud mortally ill and gave him the assistance and consolations of the Holy Church. Shortly after, he began to sink under the inexorable attacks of the plague. He had foreseen this and had telegraphed the Archbishop of New Orleans, requesting two priests.

A Jesuit father and an assistant from the cathedral left on October 3rd; they arrived soon enough to console him in his last moments and to open heaven to him. He died on the 8th, having completed his fortieth year in the eighteenth year of his priesthood.

Gentlemen, I have often spoken to you of the growing prosperity of my mission and its hopes for the future. Today I have told you of the losses and the sorrows. The hand of God has struck me, and with these priests, pride of the priesthood, the crown of my old age has fallen. Inscrutable, truly, are the ways of the Lord. I adore them and I accept them with my whole soul, and I can only say: Happy is the diocese that could lose such men, happy is the earth watered by their sweat and sanctified by their death. Martyrs to charity or martyrs to persecution, in their venerated tombs will grow the deepest roots of the Holy Church of the One whose death was our life.

Pray, gentlemen, that before my own death, I may find worthy successors to the ministry and the admirable virtues of these saintly priests.

Aug. Marie, Bishop of Natchitoches

On February 3, 1876, a lengthy procession formed before Holy Trinity Church, despite it being a busy Thursday morning. Business would wait on this day. With a cross-bearer leading them, the group of parishioners, joined by many other citizens, walked toward City Cemetery six blocks away to collect the mortal remains of their first vicar, Father Isidore Quémerais. It was determined that he was also to rest under the sanctuary of the church, next to his pastor Father Pierre and Father François Le Vézouët, the final of the five heroic priests to sacrifice their lives in the epidemic.

With the pastor of Holy Trinity, Father Joseph Gentille, leading the way, the coffin containing the body of Father Isidore Quémerais was reverently placed on a bier. Along the way back to the church from the City Cemetery, the people of Shreveport paused on downtown streets, moved by the public procession and pausing to remember the reason for it. Then a solemn Mass of Requiem was offered, sung by the students of Saint Vincent's Academy. Officiating was Reverend Father Joseph Aubree of Many, Louisiana; Reverend Father Tom Laughery of Marshall, Texas, acting deacon; and Reverend Father V. Pellonin of Shreveport, sub-deacon, with Reverend Father Hennessy of Jefferson, Texas, orator of the day.[136]

With every appropriate honor given him, Father Quémerais was placed below the high altar, directly next to his pastor and mentor, Father Jean Pierre. Eight years later, the remains of three of the five priests would be moved to the new Catholic Cemetery in town, and importantly, Father

Jean Pierre and his assistant who served such a brief time, Father Isidore Quémerais, would continue to rest side by side.

March 1884 witnessed the second transfer of their remains, and at this point, the three priests had been buried beneath Holy Trinity's altar together for many years. Again, under the watchful eye of Father Joseph Gentille, the work to exhume the remains for reburial at Saint Joseph Cemetery commenced. When approaching the grave of Father Jean Pierre, it took great effort to lift the iron casket from the tomb, and as the coffin was freed from the earth, water was heard sloshing inside and was soon witnessed seeping from its crevices. The four men strained to turn the casket head up. Water then rushed out and emptied back into the grave below. The coffin was noted to be in good condition.

At ten o'clock the following morning, the workers gathered again to open the grave beneath Holy Trinity containing Father Isidore Quémerais. His wooden coffin, found decaying but somewhat intact, was removed with equal reverence. The men transferred his remains to a new coffin. The women of the Ladies Altar Society of Holy Trinity gathered and spent the day lavishly decorating the church for another greatly anticipated High Requiem Mass.[137]

Perhaps appropriately reminiscent of the incessant rains of the summer and fall of 1873, on this day, thunderstorms brought torrents of rain beginning around one-thirty in the morning on Saturday, March 22. The streets were temporarily flooded and quickly turned to muck in the areas where there were yet no brick pavers installed. Then, at six o'clock, an early morning rainbow shone brightly, signaling an end to the showers that again threatened to delay the ceremonies. Father Gentille began Mass promptly at seven o'clock with the congregation crowded in the church. Two new wooden caskets flanked Father Pierre's cleaned but original iron sarcophagus.[138]

At ten o'clock, the cortege solemnly commenced, with Father Gentille following four altar boys. The first carried Holy Trinity's processional cross; the three behind him carried crosses bound for the priests' new tombs. The caskets of the yellow fever martyrs to their charity were conveyed behind the priests in attendance. Joining the procession were the Sisters of Saint Mary's Academy and of Saint Vincent's, along with more than twenty carriages of laymen and women. This solemn procession covered more than two miles along the Texas Road through intermittent showers and reached the new Catholic Cemetery gates at eleven o'clock, where three empty tombs awaited the reception of the martyred remains. Father Gentille was assisted by Father Napoleon Joseph Rolleaux, and the pair blessed each vault in

Stained-glass window at Holy Trinity Church in Shreveport, Louisiana, showing the detail of the five Servants of God. *Authors' collection.*

succession. Father Gentille expressed the heartfelt thanks of the people of Shreveport for the priests' lives of selfless ministry. The caskets were gently lowered into their brick, stone and cement tombs. Then, through the length of another rain shower, the brickmasons went to work sealing the tombs.[139] The diary of Father Joseph Gentille provides the details of the ceremony, making special note of "the piety of the local devoted faithful."[140]

On each major commemorative year, there have been Memorial Masses held at Holy Trinity Church specifically in honor of these five priests: the 25th anniversary in 1898, the 50th anniversary in 1923, the 75th anniversary in 1948 (occasioned with beginning the installation of stained-glass windows at Holy Trinity), the 100th anniversary in 1973, the 125th anniversary in 1998 and the 150th anniversary in 2023. Many of the intervening years, not even coinciding with specific, significant anniversary festivities, have been replete with public occasions to commemorate these five priests.[141]

On November 17, 1906, marking the thirty-third anniversary of the yellow fever epidemic, the *Shreveport Journal* again recounted the sacrifice of Father Jean Pierre and the others by noting, "In this brief period [of the epidemic], five priests braved death and willingly gave up their lives at duty's call." A 1935 Shreveport historical article refers to their sacrifice this way: "During the prevalence of the epidemic, five Catholic priests, in the active discharge of their holy duty, died victims of the disease." In 1963, printed editions of public remembrance ceremonies refer to them as "this heroic brotherhood." The 1973 centennial publication of the yellow fever epidemic was headlined, "Their Sacrifice Commemorated: The Final Roll Call, No Greater Love!"[142]

In 1986, when the United States National Park Service recognized Holy Trinity by placing it on the National Register of Historic Places, the following supporting evidence for the designation appeared in the "Statement of Significance," specifically related to Father Jean Pierre but noting also the other four priests:

> *In 1857, Father Jean Pierre oversaw construction of the first Holy Trinity Church. This frame structure on Milam Street was superseded in 1858 by a new brick church built on the present site. Father Pierre's work in Shreveport continued until his untimely death during the yellow fever epidemic of 1873. This period of crisis presented the greatest challenge to the fledgling Catholic community. In the course of less than four weeks in September to October 1873, five Catholics priests died in their efforts to aid the stricken Shreveport population.[143]*

Therefore, it was the sacrificial story of Father Jean Pierre and the other four priests—only one of whom actually served at Holy Trinity yet all of whom are associated so inextricably with its history—that helped support and merit this esteemed national recognition. Supporting architectural documents specifically highlight the west nave windows dedicated to the five priests. In addition to the National Park Service recognition of 1984, the State of Louisiana has also designated Holy Trinity a state historic site based on its architectural, cultural and historical significance, also observing in its public significance documents, "Five of its priests lost their lives treating the victims of the Yellow Fever Epidemic of 1873."[144]

In 1896, when the third Holy Trinity Church was constructed on the same site of the second one that Father Pierre built, the central stained-glass window over the altar was dedicated to his memory. This window, made of Munich glass and installed sometime between 1896 and 1903, depicts a scene of the Holy Trinity and frames the entire central architectural focal point of the church. By 1949, Holy Trinity Church had installed stained-glass windows in the west nave in honor of the five priests, with Father Jean

The earliest known photograph of the five Shreveport Servants of God. This composite image was produced in the 1870s by local photographer J.H.C. Ahrens, presumably from known images of each priest. *Authors' collection.*

The stained-glass windows at Holy Trinity Church in Shreveport that were installed in the era immediately after World War II. They provide evidence of ongoing devotion and remembrance of the Shreveport Martyrs' sacrifice. *Authors' collection.*

Pierre in the center. Similarly, devoted Catholics of the broader community also raised funds to paint a mural of him and the other four Servants of God on the ceiling of that church.[145]

A devotion to Father Jean Pierre has since come to extend beyond the boundaries of the Diocese of Shreveport, the state of Louisiana and, indeed, the United States. A reception held in Lanloup, France, in February 2019 revealed a rare civic and ecclesiastical unity for his remembrance. Again, on April 24, 2022 (the Second Sunday of Easter, Divine Mercy Sunday), on the occasion of a delegation visit to Lanloup by members of the Historical Commission for the Cause of Beatification and Canonization, there was a commemorative Mass offered at the Church of Sant-Loup. The Vicar General of the Diocese of Saint-Brieuc et Tréguier served as the principal celebrant:

> *Mass in honor of five missionary Breton priests, martyrs to their charity, including Father Jean Pierre of Lanloup, who travelled to Louisiana to evangelize in 1854, and in 1873, aided the population suffering from yellow fever to the point of giving their lives.*[146]

Illustration from the graphic novel produced about the Shreveport Martyrs by Deacon Andrew Thomas, based on the narrative provided by Father Peter B. Mangum, W. Ryan Smith and Dr. Cheryl White. *Authors' collection.*

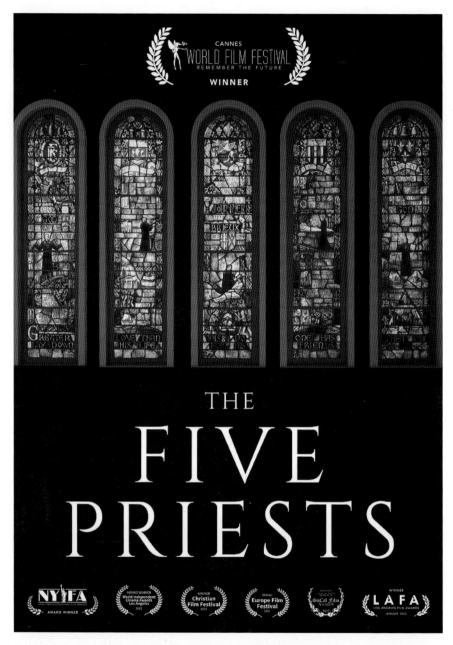

Poster for the award-winning feature documentary *The Five Priests*, which won awards at over three dozen international film festivals. The film documents the life and sacrifice of Father Jean Pierre and the other four Shreveport Martyrs. *Authors' collection.*

Left: Father Louis Gergaud of Saint Matthew's Church in Monroe, Louisiana, the fourth of the five Shreveport Martyrs to die. *Diocese of Alexandria Archives Collection.*

Right: Grave ledger installed in 2022 at the burial site of Father Jean Pierre in St. Joseph Cemetery, describing him as "Servant of God." *Authors' collection.*

Beyond beautiful tombs, stained glass, murals, prayer cards and fitting public tributes, together, the five priests of the 1873 yellow fever epidemic found ever younger audiences with a graphic novel, *Shreveport Martyrs*, artistically rendered by Deacon Andrew Thomas. Furthermore, a feature-length documentary film, *The Five Priests*, won international acclaim, highlighting their inextricably linked stories for a global audience.

It is from this rich memorial narrative that an obvious historical observation emerges. The story of Father Jean Pierre's life and sacrificial death cannot be fully told in isolation from the "heroic brotherhood" of the four other priests who shared his unwavering commitment—and his fate. Today, four of the five priests are now buried together in Shreveport's Saint Joseph Cemetery. Resting alongside Father Pierre are his assistant, Father Isidore Quémerais; Father Jean Marie Biler; and Father François Le Vézouët.

Father Louis Gergaud is now buried in Saint Matthew's Cemetery in Monroe, Louisiana.

Calvary Mound at St. Joseph Cemetery in Shreveport, where four of the five Shreveport Martyrs are buried. *Authors' collection.*

In June 2022, the graves of these priests received new memorial ledgers with epitaphs that recognize their current status as Servants of God. Also as of 2022, in a historic move by the Dicastery for the Causes of Saints in Rome, all five Servants of God will proceed henceforth as a single Cause.[147] They were united in priestly ministry on earth, committed together to selfless charity, and are now united in eternity.

Requiescat in pace.

Inscrutable, truly, are the ways of the Lord. I adore them and I accept them with my whole soul, and I can only say: Happy is the diocese that could lose such men, happy is the earth watered by their sweat and sanctified by their death. Martyrs to charity or martyrs to persecution, in their venerated tombs will grow the deepest roots of the Holy Church of the One whose death was our life.[148]

NOTES

Chapter 1

1. Mathisen, "Barbarian Bishops."
2. Diocese of Saint Brieuc et Tréguier, Archives, seminary records of Jean Pierre.
3. Diocese of Saint Brieuc et Tréguier, Archives.
4. University of Notre Dame, South Bend, Indiana, Archives, Diocese of Natchitoches Collection.
5. Annals of the Propagation of the Faith, January 1855.
6. Diocese of Saint Brieuc et Tréguier, Archives.
7. d'Antoni, "Bayou Pierre."
8. Diocese of Saint Brieuc et Tréguier, Archives.
9. University of Notre Dame, South Bend, Indiana, Archives, Diocese of Natchitoches Collection.
10. University of Notre Dame, South Bend, Indiana, Archives, Diocese of Natchitoches Collection.
11. Archdiocese of New Orleans, Louisiana, Archives and Collections.
12. University of Notre Dame, South Bend, Indiana, Archives, Diocese of Natchitoches Collection.
13. University of Notre Dame, South Bend, Indiana, Archives, Diocese of Natchitoches Collection.
14. University of Notre Dame, South Bend, Indiana, Archives, Diocese of Natchitoches Collection.

15. Brock, "Rock Chapel Ministered."

16. O'Pry, *Chronicles of Shreveport*, 322.

17. This was the description Rear Admiral David Porter gave of the Red River in official reports made during the Union's Red River Campaign in the Civil War. The Union objective was to capture and occupy the city of Shreveport as the economic gateway to Texas.

18. Tyson, *Red River*, 94.

19. Natchitoches Parish, Louisiana, *Conveyance Record Book 24*.

20. O'Pry, *Chronicles of Shreveport*, 188.

21. Tyson, *Red River*, 22–25.

22. Colonial Dames, *Historical Profile of Shreveport*, 3.

23. *New Orleans Times Picayune*, as cited by the Colonial Dames, *Historical Profiles of Shreveport*, 5–6.

24. Colonial Dames, *Historical Profiles of Shreveport*, 6–7.

25. United States Census, 1860.

26. United States Census, 1860.

27. Howard Association, *Report of the Committee*, 12.

28. Booth, *Inaugural Dissertation*, 12; *Boston Medical and Surgical Journal* 90, 73; Howard Association, *Report of the Committee*, 6.

29. University of Notre Dame, South Bend, Indiana, Archives, Diocese of Natchitoches Collection.

30. University of Notre Dame, South Bend, Indiana, Archives, Diocese of Natchitoches Collection.

31. City of Shreveport Map, 1872.

32. Texas State Historical Association, *Handbook of Tejano History*.

33. The current church is located at the intersection of Fannin and Marshall Streets. Again, "Fannin" bore great historical significance, identified as it was with James Walker Fannin, who served in the Texian army that surrendered to Mexican forces and was subsequently executed at Goliad in 1836.

34. Holy Trinity Church (Shreveport, Louisiana), Sacramental Registers.

35. Diocese of Natchitoches Collection, University of Notre Dame Archives, South Bend, Indiana.

36. Correspondence of Father Jean Pierre to Bishop Auguste Martin, Archives of the Diocese of Alexandria, Louisiana.

37. Correspondence of Father Jean Pierre to Bishop Auguste Martin, Archives of the Diocese of Alexandria, Louisiana.

38. *Shreveport Times*, January 9, 1868.

39. University of Notre Dame, South Bend, Indiana, Archives, Diocese of Natchitoches Collection.

Chapter 2

40. Saucier, *History of Avoyelles Parish*, 51.
41. Second Plenary Council of Baltimore, Proceedings.

Chapter 3

42. Booth, *Inaugural Dissertation*, 6–7.
43. Booth, *Inaugural Dissertation*, 6–7.
44. Johnson, "Great Yellow Fever Epidemic," 97.
45. *Boston Medical and Surgical Journal* 90, 73.
46. Augustine Booth, in his medical dissertation, refers to "the withering hand of political adventurers."
47. Currie's Spring was located south of the downtown business district and named for Andrew Currie, a parishioner of Holy Trinity Church and a future mayor of Shreveport. Even those willing to walk the distance to the spring could not always afford the cost of the water.
48. There are some surviving examples of such cisterns, including one at the Bridges-McKellar mansion west of downtown. Perhaps one of the best examples is still located at 209 Texas Street, which in 1873 housed the medical practice of Dr. Joseph Moore and Lewis Druggists. This was, ironically, a heavily trafficked area for yellow fever victims seeking treatment or medicines for the malady.
49. *Daily Shreveport Times*, August 20, 1873.
50. There had been outbreaks of yellow fever in 1837 and 1845 (which claimed the lives of Shreveport pioneers William Bennett and James Cane), as well as a more significant outbreak that occurred in 1853, the same one that devastated the city of New Orleans.
51. *Daily Shreveport Times*, August 12, 1873.
52. *Daily Shreveport Times*, August 21 and 22, 1873.
53. Diocese of Natchitoches Collection, University of Notre Dame Archives, South Bend, Indiana.
54. According to popular hagiography, this is believed to be Saint Lupus of Troyes, a fourth-century bishop, for whom an early popular devotion developed, especially noted throughout the Brittany region of France.
55. The Memorial of St. Blaise is celebrated on February 3. The formula for the blessing remains largely unchanged across the centuries and is one of the Church's most enduring historical traditions of combatting illnesses.

56. Butler, *Lives of the Saints*, 301.

57. Matthew 19:27–29.

58. Holy Trinity Church (Shreveport, Louisiana), Sacramental Registers.

59. Correspondence of Bishop Auguste Martin, Diocese of Natchitoches Collection, University of Notre Dame Archives, South Bend, Indiana.

60. *Daily Shreveport Times*, September 2, 1873; *New Orleans Medical and Surgical Journal* 13, 169; *Boston Medical and Surgical Journal* 90, 74.

61. Booth, *Inaugural Dissertation*, 12.

62. *Daily Shreveport Times*, August 25, 1873, and September 2, 1873.

63. *Daily Shreveport Times*, November 15, 1873.

64. The body of Leopold Baer was returned to Shreveport for burial in Hebrew Rest, located within the old City Cemetery (today Oakland Cemetery) in 1905.

65. *Daily Shreveport Times*, September 2, 1873.

66. *Daily Shreveport Times*, November 15, 1873.

67. *Daily Shreveport Times*, November 15, 1873.

68. Gentille, personal diary.

69. Le Conniat, correspondence with Bishop Auguste Martin.

70. *Daily Shreveport Times*, November 15, 1873.

71. Crosby, *American Plague*, 56.

72. *Daily Shreveport Times*, September 2, 1873.

73. *Daily Shreveport Times*, September 7, 1873.

74. *Daily Shreveport Times*, September 3, 1873.

75. *Daily Shreveport Times*, September 4, 1873.

76. *Daily Shreveport Times*, September 4, 1873.

77. *Daily Shreveport Times*, September 4, 1873.

78. *Daily Shreveport Times*, November 15, 1873.

79. *Daily Shreveport Times*, September 4, 1873; United States Census, 1870. The Howard Association used a modified version of the police jury city wards to organize its relief efforts. Fever Ward 1 does not appear to completely align with the U.S. Census Bureau's Ward Number 1, however. Ward 1 was the least populated ward in the 1870 census, while the opposite is likely true of the wards determined by the Howard Association (Gary D. Joiner, 2018).

80. *Daily Shreveport Times*, November 15, 1873.

81. *Daily Shreveport Times*, November 15, 1873.

82. *Daily Shreveport Times*, September 4, 1873.

83. *Daily Shreveport Times*, September 5, 1873.

84. *Daily Shreveport Times*, September 5, 1873.

85. *Daily Shreveport Times*, September 6, 1873.

86. Quoted in d'Antoni, Calendar of Letters. The original letter has not been located in the files; this reference is from a secondary account.

87. *Daily Shreveport Times*, September 5 and 6, 1873.

88. *Shreveport Journal*, June 27, 1935.

89. *New York Times*, October 15, 1873.

90. Holy Trinity Church (Shreveport, Louisiana), Sacramental Registers.

91. *Daily Shreveport Times*, September 9 and 10, 1873.

92. McCants, *They Came to Louisiana*, 223.

93. Le Conniat, correspondence.

94. Elford, "Brief History."

95. *Daily Shreveport Times*, November 15, 1873.

96. *Daily Shreveport Times*, November 15, 1873.

97. *Daily Shreveport Times*, June 27, 1935.

98. Woodruff, personal letter.

99. Le Conniat, correspondence.

100. Le Conniat, correspondence.

101. Martin, correspondence; Le Conniat, correspondence.

102. Daughters of the Cross, Register.

103. Daughters of the Cross, Register.

104. *Daily Shreveport Times*, September 11, 1873.

105. *Daily Shreveport Times*, September 13, 1873.

106. *New York Times*, September 30, 1873.

107. *Daily Shreveport Times*, September 13, 1873.

108. Le Conniat, correspondence.

109. Le Conniat, correspondence.

110. Daughters of the Cross Victims of 1873 Shreveport Yellow Fever Epidemic. Unpublished manuscript, Archives of the Diocese of Shreveport.

111. Horace, as quoted by St. Alphonsus Ligouri.

112. Le Conniat, correspondence.

113. Le Conniat, correspondence.

114. Scudder, *Eclectic Medical Journal*.

115. *Daily Shreveport Times*, September 17, 1873.

116. Martin, correspondence.

117. *Missale Romanum*.

118. "Have among yourselves the same attitude that is also yours in Christ Jesus, Who, though He was in the form of God, did not regard equality with God as something to be grasped. Rather, he emptied Himself, taking the form of a slave, coming in human likeness; and found human

in appearance, he humbled Himself, becoming obedient to death, even death on a cross. Because of this, God greatly exalted Him and bestowed on Him the name that is above every name, that at the name of Jesus every knee should bend, of those in heaven and on earth and under the earth, and every tongue confess that Jesus Christ is Lord, to the glory of God the Father." (Philippians 2:5–11).

119. Le Conniat, correspondence.

120. Le Conniat, correspondence.

121. Le Conniat, correspondence.

122. Scudder, *Eclectic Medical Journal*.

123. Le Conniat, correspondence.

124. Le Conniat, correspondence.

125. Diocese of Shreveport, Louisiana, Archives.

126. Le Conniat, correspondence.

127. Le Conniat, correspondence.

128. Le Conniat, correspondence.

Chapter 4

129. *Daily Shreveport Times*, September 17, 1873.

130. Correspondence of Bishop Auguste Martin.

131. *Daily Shreveport Times*, November 15, 1873.

132. Correspondence of Bishop Auguste Martin.

133. *Daily Shreveport Times*, September 17, 1873.

134. *Daily Shreveport Times*, September 18, 1873.

135. Martin, correspondence.

136. Gentille, personal diary; *Shreveport Times*, February 6, 1873; *Morning Star and Catholic Messenger*, February 13, 1876.

137. Gentille, personal diary; Diocese of Shreveport, Louisiana, Archives.

138. Gentille, personal diary.

139. Gentille, personal diary.

140. Gentille, personal diary.

141. Sacramental Registers of Holy Trinity Church, Shreveport, Louisiana.

142. *Shreveport Times*; *Shreveport Journal*.

143. National Park Service, Statement of Significance, Holy Trinity Church in Shreveport, Louisiana.

144. Louisiana Department of Culture, Recreation and Tourism, State of Louisiana Historical Commemorations.

145. Sacramental Registers of Holy Trinity Church.
146. Diocese of St. Brieuc et Tréguier Archives, Church of Sant Loup, Lanloup, France.
147. Dicastery for the Causes of Saints.
148. Martin, correspondence.

BIBLIOGRAPHY

Allen, Francis R. "Development of the Public Health Movement in the Southeast." *Social Forces* 22, no. 1 (1904).

American Association for the Advancement of Science. "Symposium on Yellow Fever and Other Insect Borne Diseases." *Science* 23, no. 58 (March 1906).

———. "Yellow Fever and Mosquitoes." *Science* 12, no. 305 (November 1900).

American Catholic Historical Society. "Southern Historical Notes." *American Catholic Historical Researches*, New Series 2, no. 2 (1906).

American Church Almanac and Yearbook: 1898–1899. James Pott, 1911.

Annals of the Propagation of the Faith, Paris, France.

Archdiocese of New Orleans, Louisiana, Archives and Collections.

Archdiocese of Rennes, France, Archives.

Baudier Historical Collection 23 (Heroes of '73). Archives of the Archdiocese of New Orleans.

Bell, A.N., ed. *The Sanitarian: A Monthly Magazine Dedicated to the Preservation of Health, Mental and Physical Culture.* Vol. 2 (1874).

Biever, Albert H. *The Jesuits in New Orleans and the Mississippi Valley: Jubilee Memorial.* Society of Jesus, 1924.

Blanc, Archbishop Antoine. Correspondence. Archives of the University of Notre Dame, South Bend, Indiana.

Booth, Augustine R. *An Inaugural Dissertation on the History of the Epidemic of Shreveport, Louisiana.* University of Kentucky Medical School, 1873.

Boston Medical and Surgical Journal. Vol. 90, 1890.

Boyce, Robert William. *Yellow Fever and Its Prevention: A Manual for Medical Students and Practitioners.* E.P. Dutton, 1911.

Breeden, James O. "Joseph Jones and Public Health in the New South." *Louisiana History: The Journal of the Louisiana Historical Association* 32, no. 4 (August 1991).

Brock, Eric. "Rock Chapel Ministered to Post-Slavery Blacks." *Shreveport Times*, December 19, 1998.

Brock, Eric J. *Shreveport.* Pelican Publishing, 2001.

———. *Shreveport Chronicles: Profiles from Louisiana's Port City.* The History Press, 2009.

Butler, Father Alban. *Lives of the Saints.* Tan Book Publishers, 1994.

Carrigan, JoAnn. *The Saffron Scourge: A History of Yellow Fever in Louisiana, 1796–1905.* University of Southwestern Louisiana Press, 1994.

Carroll, James, William C. Gorgas, Robert L. Owen and Walter D. McCaw. *Yellow Fever: A Compilation of Various Publications.* United States Government Printing Office, 1911.

Carter, Henry Rose. *Yellow Fever: An Epidemiological and Historical Study of Its Place of Origin.* Williams and Wilkins, 1931.

Catholic Encyclopedia. Robert Appleton, 1917.

Catholic News Messenger (New Orleans, LA).

Catholic Propagator (New Orleans, LA).

Chicago Tribune.

Christophers, Sir S. Rickard. *Aedes Aegypti: The Yellow Fever Mosquito, Its Life History, Bionomics and Structure.* Cambridge University Press, 1960.

City of Shreveport Map, 1872.

The Clinic (Cincinnati, OH). January 10, 1874.

Coleman, William L. *A History of Yellow Fever: Indisputable Facts, Origin and Cause.* Clinic Publishing, 1898.

Colonial Dames. *Historical Profile of Shreveport.* Self-published, 1850.

Crosby, Mary Caldwell. *The American Plague: The Untold Story of Yellow Fever, the Epidemic That Shaped Our History.* Berkeley Books, 2006.

Dabbs, James Muse. Letters. Ouachita Parish Louisiana History. https://ouachitaparishhistory.com.

Daily Shreveport Times (Shreveport, LA).

d'Antoni, Blaise. "Bayou Pierre: Land of Yesteryear." Unpublished manuscript. Archives of the Archdiocese of New Orleans, 1958.

———. Calendar of Letters. University of Notre Dame Archives, South Bend, Indiana.

d'Antoni, Blaise G. "Bayou Pierre, Land of Yesteryear: A Sesquicentennial History of Immaculate Conception Chapel of Carmel and the Church of the Holy Apostles of Bayou Pierre, 1808–1958." Unpublished manuscript. Archives of the Diocese of Shreveport, Louisiana, and the Archives of the Archdiocese of New Orleans.

Daughters of the Cross. Register. Archives of the Diocese of Shreveport, Louisiana.

———. "Victims of 1873 Yellow Fever Epidemic." Unpublished manuscript. Archives of the Diocese of Shreveport, Louisiana.

Dicastery for the Causes of Saints. Rome, Italy.

Diocese of Alexandria Archives. Alexandria, Louisiana.

Diocese of Shreveport, Louisiana, Archives.

Diocese of St. Brieuc et Treguier, France, Archives.

Doughty, Edward. *Observations and Inquiries into the Nature and Treatment of Yellow, or Bulam, Fever.* Highley and Sons, 1816.

Duffy, J. "Yellow Fever in the Continental United States in the Nineteenth Century." *Bulletin of the New York Academy of Medicine* 44 (June 1968): 687–701.

Dumas, Antoine, and Jean Deshusses, eds. *Liber Sacramentorum Gellonensis.* Brepols Publishing, 1981.

Elford, Madeline. "A Brief History of St. Vincent's Academy and Daughters of the Cross." Unpublished manuscript. Archives of the Diocese of Shreveport, Louisiana.

Espinosa, Mariola. "The Question of Racial Immunity to Yellow Fever in History and Historiography." *Social Science History* 38, nos. 3–4 (Fall/Winter 2014).

Ford, W. Hutson. *Reports to the St. Louis Medical Society on Yellow Fever.* George Rumbold, 1878.

Frank Leslie's Illustrated Newspaper (New York, NY).

Garvey, Joan B., and Mary Lou Widmer. *Beautiful Cresent: A History of New Orleans.* Pelican Publishing, 2013.

Gentille, Father Joseph. Personal diary. Archives of the Diocese of Shreveport, Louisiana.

Goodyear, James D. "The Sugar Connection: A New Perspective on the History of Yellow Fever." *Bulletin of the History of Medicine* 52, no. 1 (Spring 1978).

Gudmestad, Robert. *Steamboats and the Rise of the Cotton Kingdom.* Louisiana State University Press, 2011.

Hale, W. Chris, Gary D. Joiner, Bernadette Palombo and Cheryl H. White. *Wicked Shreveport.* The History Press, 2011.

Hall, Judge Henry Gerard. Personal diary. Noel Archives and Special Collections, Louisiana State University at Shreveport, Shreveport, Louisiana.

Hennessey, James. "The First Vatican Council." *Archivium Historiae Pontificiae* 7 (1969), 38.

Hildreth, Peggy Bassett. "Early Red Cross: The Howard Association of New Orleans, 1837–1878." *Louisiana History: The Journal of the Louisiana Historical Association* 20, no. 1 (Winter 1979).

Hill, Ralph N. *The Doctors Who Conquered Yellow Fever.* Random House, 1957.

Holy Trinity Church (Shreveport, Louisiana). Sacramental Registers.

———. Archives of the Diocese of Shreveport, Louisiana.

Howard Association. *Report of the Committee on the Yellow Fever Epidemic of 1873 at Shreveport, Louisiana.* Howard Association, 1874.

Howard, Leland O. *Concerning the Geographic Distribution of the Yellow Fever Mosquito.* United States Government Printing Office, 1902.

Humphreys, Margaret. *Yellow Fever and the South.* John Hopkins University Press, 1992.

Ignatius, Sister D.C. *Across Three Centuries.* Benzinger Brothers, 1932.

Jefferson (TX) Democrat.

Johnson, Margaret. "The Great Yellow Fever Epidemic of Shreveport in 1873." *North Louisiana Historical Journal* 30, no. 4 (Winter 1999): 16.

Joiner, Gary D. (professor and chair, Department of History, Louisiana State University at Shreveport). Personal interview by W. Ryan Smith, 2018.

Joiner, Gary D., and White, Cheryl H. *Shreveport's Oakland Cemetery: Spirits of Pioneers and Heroes.* The History Press, 2015.

Journal of the Telegraph (New York, NY).

Kelly, Howard Atwood. *Walter Reed and Yellow Fever.* McClure, Phillips, 1906.

Kotar, S.L., and J.E. Gessler. *Yellow Fever: A Worldwide History.* McFarland, 2017.

LaRoche, Rene. *Yellow Fever Considered in Its Historical, Pathological, Etiological, and Thermapeutical Relations.* Blanchard and Lea, 1855.

Leavity, Judith W., and Ronald L. Numbers, eds. *Sickness and Health in America: Readings in the History of Medicine and Public Health.* University of Wisconsin Press, 1997.

Le Conniat, Mother Mary Hyacinth. Correspondence. Noel Archives and Special Collections, Louisiana State University at Shreveport.

Lining, John. *Description of the American Yellow Fever in the Year 1748.* Pennsylvania Medical Society, 1799.

Louisiana Department of Culture, Recreation and Tourism, State of Louisiana Historical Commemorations.

Mahe, Reverend C. "History of the Missions of the Ouachita." Unpublished manuscript, 1929. Archives of the Archdiocese of New Orleans, Louisiana.

Martin, Bishop Auguste Marie. Annual Reports to the Society for the Propagation of the Faith, Paris, France. MPFP-096, Archives of the University of Notre Dame, South Bend, Indiana.

————. Correspondence to the Society for the Propagation of the Faith, Paris, France. MPFP-096, Archives of the University of Notre Dame, South Bend, Indiana.

————. Letters. Daughters of the Cross Collection, Noel Archives and Special Collections, Louisiana State University at Shreveport, Shreveport, Louisiana.

————. Letters. Register of the Daughters of the Cross, Archives of the Diocese of Shreveport, Louisiana.

————. "Notice on Very Rev. Father Gergaud from the Right Rev. Aug. Marie Martin, Bishop of Natchitoches." *Catholic Propagator*, November 12, 1873.

————. Personal diary (Vatican Council). Archives of the Archdiocese of New Orleans, Louisiana.

Martin, James W. *Yellow Fever: A Monograph.* Livingstone, 1892.

Mathisen, Ralph W. "Barbarian Bishops and the Churches of Late Antiquity." *Speculum* 72, no. 3 (July 1997): 31.

McCants, Sr. Dorothea Olga. *They Came to Louisiana: Letters of a Catholic Mission, 1854–1882.* Daughters of the Cross, 1983.

McLure, Mary Lilla, and Jolley Edward Howe. *History of Shreveport and Shreveport Builders.* Journal Printing, 1937.

Miciotto, Robert J. "Shreveport's First Major Health Crisis: The Yellow Fever Epidemic of 1873." *North Louisiana Historical Journal* 4, no. 4 (Fall 2016).

Missale Romanum. Archdiocese of Tours, 1869.

Nashville (TN) Union and American.

Natchitoches Parish, Louisiana. Conveyance Records. Natchitoches Parish Courthouse.

National Park Service. Statement of Significance for Holy Trinity Church, National Register of Historic Places.

New Orleans Medical and Surgical Journal 13, 169.

New Orleans Picayune.

New York Times.

New York World.

Nolan, Charles E. *Splendors of Faith: New Orleans Catholic Churches, 1727–1930.* Louisiana State University Press, 2010.

Nott, Josiah. "The Cause of Yellow Fever." *New Orleans Medical and Surgical Journal* 4 (1848).

Oldstone, Michael B. *Viruses, Plagues, and History.* Oxford University Press, 2000.

O'Pry, Maude Hearn. *Chronicles of Shreveport.* Self-published, 1928.

Ouachita Citizen (Monroe, LA).

Ouachita Telegraph (Monroe, LA).

Paine, Thomas. *Miscellaneous Letters and Essay on Various Subjects.* R. Carlile Publishing, 1819.

Partain, Fr. Chad A. *A Tool Pushed by Providence: Bishop Auguste Martin and the Catholic Church in North Louisiana.* Persidia, 2010.

Patterson, K. David. "Yellow Fever Epidemics and Mortality in the United States, 1693–1905." *Social Science and Medicine* 34, no. 8 (April 1992).

Pierce, John R., and James V. Writer. *Yellow Jack: How Yellow Fever Ravaged America and Walter Reed Discovered Its Deadly Secrets.* Wiley and Sons, 2005.

Pierre, Father Jean. Correspondence. Archives of the Diocese of Alexandria, Louisiana.

Plauche, Rt. Rev. Msgr. JV. *A Brief History of Holy Trinity Church, Shreveport, Louisiana, and of the Catholic Church in Northwest Louisiana.* Holy Trinity Church, 1942.

Radcliffe, J. "A Note on the Recurrence of Yellow Fever Epidemics in Urban Populations." *Journal of Applied Probability* 11, no. 1 (March 1974).

Rapides Gazette (Alexandria, LA).

"Report of the Committee on the Yellow Fever Epidemic of 1873 of Shreveport, Louisiana." *American Journal of the Medical Sciences* 66, no. 134 (1874): 41–44.

Sadlier's Catholic Directory, Almanac, and Ordo. D. & J. Sadlier, 1873.

Sant Loup Parish Church Sacramental Register. Lanloup, France.

Saucier, Corinne. *A History of Avoyelles Parish.* Pelican Publishing, 1943.

The Scholastic (University of Notre Dame). "Priests Who Have Died at Shreveport." 1873.

Scudder, John M., ed. *The Eclectic Medical Journal.* Self-published, 1874.

Second Plenary Council of Baltimore. Proceedings. 1866.

Seminary of St. Brieuc-Tréguier. Records. Diocese of St. Brieuc, France.

Shmaefsky, Brian. *Deadly Diseases and Epidemics: Yellow Fever.* Chelsea House Publishing, 2010.

Shreveport (LA) Journal.

Society of Jesus Central Provincial Archives. St. Louis, Missouri.

State of Louisiana Department of Culture, Recreation and Tourism. Sites of Historical Significance and Historical Markers Program.

Sternberg, George M. *Report on the Etiology and Prevention of Yellow Fever.* United States Government Printing Office, 1890.

Strode, George K. *Yellow Fever.* McGraw Hill, 1951.

Taylor, Milton W. *Viruses and Man: A History of Interactions.* Springer International, 2014.

Texas State Historical Association. *The Handbook of Tejano History.* 2016.

Toner, J.M. *Contributions to the Study of Yellow Fever: A Paper Read Before the American Public Health Association in New York on the Natural History and Distribution of Yellow Fever in the United States.* U.S. Marine Hospital Services Office, 1874.

Touatre, Just. *Yellow Fever: Clinical Notes.* New Orleans Medical and Surgical Journal Publishing, 1898.

Tyson, Carl Newton. *The Red River in Southwestern History.* University of Oklahoma Press, 1981.

United States Census. United States Census Bureau, 1860, 1870, 1880.

University of Notre Dame, South Bend, Indiana, Archives. Diocese of Natchitoches Collection.

Vital Records Registry, Lanloup, France.

Vital Records Registry, Pleine-Fougères, France.

Warner, Margaret. "Hunting the Yellow Fever Germ: The Principle and Practice of Etiological Proof in Late Nineteenth Century America." *Bulletin of the History of Medicine* 59, no. 3 (Fall 1985).

Wills, Christopher. *Yellow Fever, Black Goddess: The Co-Evolution of People and Plagues.* Perseus, 1996.

Woodruff, Lt. Eugene Augustus. Personal letter of September 9, 1873. Noel Archives and Special Collections, Louisiana State University at Shreveport.

Woodworth, John. *Annual Report of the Supervising Surgeon of the Marine Hospital Service of the United States for Fiscal Year 1874.* United States Government Printing Office, 1974.

The three authors at the Calvary Mound at St. Joseph's Cemetery on the 150th anniversary of the yellow fever epidemic in Shreveport, September 15, 2023. *Authors' collection.*

ABOUT THE AUTHORS

VERY REVEREND PETER B. MANGUM was raised in Shreveport, the oldest of five sons, parishioner of St. Jude Church in Bossier City and graduate of Christ the King School in Bossier City and Jesuit High School (now Loyola) in Shreveport. He attended Holy Trinity Seminary at the University of Dallas and then the Pontifical Gregorian University in Rome, where he remained for five years, receiving degrees in sacred theology and canon law and making numerous pilgrimages to the shrines and tombs of saints in Rome and throughout Europe. Ordained a priest in 1990, "Father Peter" is currently pastor of the Church of Jesus the Good Shepherd in Monroe, Louisiana. He has researched and actively promoted the causes of the five priests who died in Shreveport's yellow fever epidemic of 1873. In 2019, in the capacity of diocesan administrator of Shreveport, he led a "Shreveport Delegation" to Brittany, France, to the native dioceses and villages of the five Shreveport Martyrs. In 2022, as episcopal delegate for the cause of beatification and canonization, he led another delegation and expansive research initiative to Brittany for more investigation into their lives. He has visited the Dicastery for the Causes of the Saints at the Vatican on several occasions to learn more about the process of canonization as it applies to those who freely offered their lives and heroically accepted, out of Christian charity, a certain and untimely death. He coauthored two other books related to the five Shreveport Servants of God: namely, *Shreveport Martyrs of 1873: The Surest Path to Heaven* (2021) and *Shreveport Martyr Father Louis Gergaud: In His Own Words* (2023), both published by The History Press. Father Peter features prominently in the internationally acclaimed film *The Five Priests*, based on the coauthors' original research, which is now publicly available on EWTN and other global streaming platforms.

W. Ryan Smith is a native of Shreveport. A husband and father of three, he serves as the director of hospital operations at Ochsner LSU Health Shreveport, the contemporary descendant of the city's first charity hospital that was established as a direct result of the 1873 yellow fever epidemic. He worked with his staff throughout the COVID-19 pandemic, coordinating higher level of care hospital transfers, inpatient capacity management operations and outpatient COVID-19 vaccine scheduling for the region. He holds both a master of arts and a bachelor of business degree from Northwestern State University of Louisiana in Natchitoches, Louisiana, and has completed postgraduate work with both the Pennsylvania State University and Villanova University. He makes his home in Shreveport and became aware of the story of the five priests while researching the medical history of the city of Shreveport. He has served on the board of Catholic Charities of North Louisiana, is a knight of the Equestrian Order of the Holy Sepulchre of Jerusalem (a nearly one-thousand-year-old chivalrous order) and was named one of the Greater Shreveport Chamber's Young Professional Initiative's "40 Under 40" in 2018. He is a parishioner of the Cathedral of St. John Berchmans in Shreveport. Smith is the author of *Sang pour Sang*, a novel published by the University of Louisiana at Lafayette Press (2018) and coauthor of *A Haunted History of Louisiana Plantations* (The History Press, 2017), a work completed along with friend and fellow researcher Dr. Cheryl H. White. He also coauthored two other books related to the five Shreveport Servants of God: *Shreveport Martyrs of 1873: The Surest Path to Heaven* (2021) and *Shreveport Martyr Father Louis Gergaud: In His Own Words* (2023), both published by The History Press. Smith features prominently in the internationally acclaimed film *The Five Priests*, based on the coauthors' original research, which is now publicly available on EWTN and other global streaming platforms.

Cheryl H. White, PhD, is a professor of history at Louisiana State University at Shreveport, where she has taught medieval European and Christian Church history for twenty-seven years. Dr. White currently holds the distinguished Hubert Humphreys Endowed Professorship and the Yancey Strain Endowed Curatorship, which have provided many research opportunities involving the fields of Christian history and local history and the study of regional folklore, resulting in numerous peer-reviewed articles and professional academic conference presentations. The LSUS Foundation has generously supported the ongoing research initiatives related to the five Shreveport Martyrs. A passionate preservationist, Dr. White is actively engaged in historic preservation advocacy and policymaking at both the local and state levels. Dr. White is a native of northwest Louisiana, and her deep love of history was first nurtured by the rich narratives of her own home state, meaning that her research has been equally focused on stories much closer to home, many of which have been published in books and articles on regional history and folklore. It was the nexus of local history and Christian history that shaped her interest in and collaboration on extensive research into the five Shreveport martyr priests of 1873, shared with colleagues Father Peter Mangum and W. Ryan Smith. With them, she coauthored two other books related to the five Shreveport Servants of God: *Shreveport Martyrs of 1873: The Surest Path to Heaven* (2021) and *Shreveport Martyr Father Louis Gergaud: In His Own Words* (2023), both published by The History Press. White also features prominently in the internationally acclaimed film *The Five Priests*, based on the coauthors' original research, which is now publicly available on EWTN and other global streaming platforms. This is her eighth book to be published with The History Press.

Visit us at
www.historypress.com